SMALL TOWNS

YOU GOTTA LOVE 'EM

Brownsdale
POP 676

DON PETERSON

ISBN: 9781099641190
ISBN-13: 9781099641190

INTRODUCTION

This book is a collection of stories gathered over the years about community, friends, family and a couple of chance encounters mostly in small town Midwest America. Some are more newsy and were printed in a local weekly newspaper, and some were in my private collection.

I have long thought about putting them all in a book to leave a part of me behind for my family when I have gone on to the great fishing grounds in the sky.

I am deeply grateful to my daughter Colette who acted as editor for this project. I also want to thank her husband Jim who acted as the assistant editor. Without their help, it is doubtful that this book would have ever actually gotten completed. Thank you both.

And sometimes remembering will lead to a story, which makes it forever. That's what stories are for. Stories are for joining the past to the future. Stories are for those late hours in the night when you can't remember how you got from where you were to where you are. Stories are for eternity, when memory is erased, when there is nothing to remember except the story.

~Tim O'Brien | *The Things They Carried*

CONTENTS

MYSTERIOUS CASE OF MISCHIEF
AND MONKEY BUSINESS

June 2009

My wife Leone and I live on the west edge of Brownsdale. A year ago we bought the lot next to us. We decided to develop it into an area of tall prairie grasses and native wildflowers.

This past winter Leone got the idea that she wanted to have a buffalo on our "Prairie Meadow" as she calls it. After all, buffalo roamed the prairies and were actually in this area according to the book, *Mower County History*.

But of course, it couldn't be just any buffalo. Leone said it had to be a white buffalo, a spirit buffalo the Indians called them. They were supposed to bring good luck.

Our project was finally completed and erected by early May. We received many comments on it. Someone even suggested that we might wake up some morning and find teepees pitched near the buffalo. We haven't found any teepees pitched out there yet, but about a week ago when we were doing some trimming in that area, we came upon a strange sight. There, behind our wooden buffalo, was a real, genuine, perfectly shaped cow pie! Cow manure. Dung.

Where could it have come from? We knew it didn't come from our buffalo. So who, what, how? One of the first people both Leone and I thought of was a legendary Brownsdale prankster, who lives across from the school, but we cannot mention his name. However, he was quickly eliminated from our list.

As to the three most likely suspects, there was a whole lot of finger pointing (in the other direction) going on. Two of them claimed to be out of town at the time of the incident, and the third one denied any knowledge of it, whatsoever.

We think the Early Morning Coffee Bunch Planning Committee that convenes daily at the local coffee shop knows a whole lot more about this caper than they are willing to admit. One of our suspects, known to frequent this establishment, was heard to comment that he thought our buffalo looked like it felt a lot better now that he had had a good bowel movement.

We have been able to learn that a farmer who lives not too far north of Brownsdale and who raises some fine cattle, supplied the raw material for this foul deed.

Also, we have it on good authority that our local law enforcement agency declined to become involved in this strange affair.

Our personal investigation into this matter is continuing. In the meantime, I believe I will set up my trail camera to discourage further harassment of our spirit buffalo by these Night Riders.

By Don Peterson, aka "Buffalo Chips"

This was the first story that I had printed. The editor of the Meadow Area News *always had a little box telling the readers that if they had any interesting stories that we should send them to her. So one night I sat down and wrote this true event up and sent it to her with a note telling her that if she had some blank space and didn't know what to do with it, maybe she could use this. I didn't hear anything back so I figured I knew where that went. The next week, the story was in the newspaper!*

ALL THE DAYS OF OUR LIVES

December 1996

I arose later than usual on Sunday morning, as is my custom. The sun was almost up. While I waited for my tea to boil, (another Sunday morning custom) I checked outside to see what kind of day we were going to have. It was "small town, Sunday morning quiet", just the way I like it.

Day was beginning to break in the east, and there were a few scattered clouds low on the horizon. It looked like it was going to be a beautiful sunrise.

My tea was done, so I carried it to a chair by the window to watch the sunrise. I was not disappointed! As I sat sipping my steaming hot, delicious early morning tea, I enjoyed nature's show.

The eastern sky slowly came alive with brilliant color! Vivid shades of yellow, pink, scarlet, red! The colors changed, sometimes seeming to blend together, then separating, always changing, almost like a dance of the colors. It was a beautiful sight that I almost missed.

Then, slowly, silently---not kicking and screaming like a newborn child, this large, bright, reddish-yellow disc slid up out of Mother Earth; and a new day was born!

You will have to use your imagination to paint in the colors.

I wondered, who else had seen and enjoyed the birth of this new day? Most of the people in my small town were still sleeping on a Sunday morning. And elsewhere? Was anyone looking? If you don't take the time to watch the birth of a new day, you miss it, since it only lasts a few seconds.

And then I thought about all the days of our lives. Each of these days lasts such a short time. And when they are gone, they are gone forever.

"Dear Lord," I thought, "how many days of my life have slipped by, unseen, unappreciated, because I was too busy?

Too busy working, struggling, surviving, coping?"

I resolved then and there not to let another day of my life slip by....unseen.

He is happiest, be he king or peasant, who finds peace in his home. ~Johann Von Goethe

AN EARLY MORNING EXPERIENCE

July 2012

Thursday morning Leone and I started out for our walk. We try to do it early, before it gets too hot, the day gets busy, etc. Usually somewhere between 5:30 am and 6:00 am. I guess we are of the old school of early to bed and early to rise. And no, we are not wealthy and sometimes I question my wisdom. But, I digress from my story.

As we approached Mower County Highway 2 going west out of Brownsdale we crossed paths with an individual walking west, pulling a two-wheeled cart. He had a blinking red light hanging around his neck and another one attached to the rear of the cart. It was foggy and not quite light yet. We said good morning to him and he responded in kind.

We knew he was a stranger passing through our town. Leone asked him if he had had breakfast yet. I knew she was trying to lure him back to our house, so we could learn more about this interesting person. He said he had, as he kept walking. This guy could really walk! I raised my voice a bit to ask him where he was from as the distance between us was widening. "Michigan," he replied. "Where are you headed?" I asked, thinking I would like to get his story. "Kansas," he replied. Not much of a talker.

As we continued on, I mentioned to Leone that I sure wish I had my camera with me, and she urged me to turn around and run back home to get it. A good idea but we were more than two blocks from home and our walker was disappearing in the fog ahead of us. I did run (uff da), got the car, camera, and something to write on and headed out. I caught up with him on Akkerman's corner (as we small town folk identify locations).

I jumped out of the car ahead of him with my camera and as he approached I asked him if I could take his picture. The conversation went something like this:

> "Can I take your picture?"
> "No, are you with a newspaper?"
> "Yes."
> "I don't do interviews."
> "Why not?"
> "I stopped doing them a long time ago."
> "Why are you doing this?" I asked, hoping to get something for my efforts.
> "Walking is a basic form of transportation," he replied, as he started to disappear in the fog ahead of me, again.

Sigh.

Sometimes our best efforts……..

The joy of living is his, who has the heart to demand it.
~Teddy Roosevelt

BROWNSDALE BITS

I have heard that it takes older people longer to get things done. The other day I think I figured out why.

I was headed outside to do some work in the yard, or as it is sometimes called in this part of the country at this time of the year, "getting ready for winter". As I opened the door, I remembered that Leone had asked me yesterday to replace a burnt out bulb in her china cupboard.

I turned around, went downstairs to look through my light bulb supply. I found the bulb and was about to open the china cupboard door when I noticed a sconce hanging on the wall that was about to slide off the nail it was on. I carefully lifted it off its hanger to place it on the counter until I could fix that problem, still holding the lightbulb in my other hand. As I did so, the glass candle holder started to wobble and finally fell off, hitting the floor with a loud crash, broken glass flying everywhere.

I was grateful that the only comment from Leone was, "That was Fostoria."

I put the bulb down and went for the broom and dustpan. Naturally, there were a couple small rugs that were sprayed with broken glass also, so I carefully folded them up and took them out for a good shaking. I then got the vacuum cleaner out and vacuumed a wide area to make sure I got all the glass splinters, and then I went outside to get the rugs and vacuum them also. As I was returning the vacuum to the closet I noticed that the vacuum cleaner bag needed to be emptied, so I did that before putting it away.

I *finally* got outside to start working on my project. It was only a very short time before Leone opened the door and said, "Dinner will be ready in about five minutes"....

———•••——

This is the "political season", isn't it? Many claims, promises and accusations. The election is over and we can settle back to normal. Nothing of much substance accomplished. All smoke and no fire? Or as they say in Texas, "Big hat, no cattle"? So sad. Anyone in favor of term limits?

All these candidates on TV every night reminded me of one thing that was accomplished in our state legislature this spring. The legislature passed a bill legalizing medical marijuana that was quickly signed into law by our governor, naturally. Afterward our Senator Dan Sparks was quoted in the *Austin Daily Herald* saying, "It is nice to be able to do something for people with chronic pain."

This got me to thinking. I am 77 years old and something hurts somewhere in my body almost every day. Does that qualify as chronic pain? Hmm, I wonder if I can get a prescription for medical marijuana? Is that covered under Medicare? Hmm, I better look into this!

———•••———

I wonder if many other people are as disgusted with the loss of our recycle bin as I am? It was so handy to just grab some things to recycle and drop them off on the way to the post office or whatever. Now we have to remember which days the county truck comes around. The second and fourth Tuesdays of the month beginning with the Tuesday of the second full week of the month. Takes a while to get used to that. And all because of a few people with no respect for the law, no self-respect, and no community pride who were using the recycle bin as a dumping ground. I wonder what they will be teaching their children? Oh, trust me on this, they will breed.

———•••———

I like to bake bread when I get the time, but it seems like I always have trouble keeping it fresh until I have it eaten up. I know our son Jason bakes bread also, so when he called the other day I asked him how he stored his bread to keep it fresh. His reply was, "Well, if it is good bread, I don't have any problem with storage." Smart aleck.

———•••———

The winter has been quite hard on me and, I suspect, on others as well. Recently I bought a new pair of dress pants. They were one size larger than what I usually wear, but I liked the color and they were on sale. I knew Leone could take them in. She is very handy with a needle and thread. When I got home, I tried on the pants so she could see how much she needed to take them in. They fit fine, no need to take them in. *Sigh*. Like I said, winter has been hard on me.

———•••———

11

I took Leone to the historic Paramount Theatre in Austin for a live performance by the Northwestern Singers of Austin. It was their winter concert. We had seats way down in the front row on the left hand side. Right where Leone likes to sit. Sitting in the Amen corner, I call it.

As we were getting seated, I reminded her that when we were teenagers I used to bring her to movies here. "Way back then you used to like to sit up in the balcony," I said. "Now you want to sit right down in the front." She didn't reply, just smiled at me with a little twinkle in her eye as she sat down.

———

My friend Dick has always been a trickster and a jokester. Unfortunately, he is now past 80 and has some dementia setting in. He may have trouble remembering some things but I know that the old Dick is still in there, somewhere.

Dick and his wife recently celebrated their 63rd anniversary. I asked him how she ever put up with him for that long. "I don't know. Why don't you ask her and then tell me so I can know too," he replied.

We went on a drive together. I asked him if he knew where we were. He said he was with me. I told him that when we get up to that T intersection ahead, if we turn right we will go to Owatonna. If we turn left we would go past the old Monterey Dance Hall.

I asked him if he remembered that place. "Oh yes," he replied, "before I was married that used to be a good place to go shopping. A lot of guys did, but I don't think it was just guys that did some shopping there." (I will leave it to you, dear reader, to figure out what they were "shopping" for.)

Coming home we went past a farm where both of us knew who used to live there, but we couldn't remember his name. I said, "I remember he was awfully tight with his money and most likely had a lot of money when he died." Dick's response was "He told me he was going to spend it all over hell." Ahhh, Dick.

In a small town church, everyone pretty well knows everyone else. An example of that is a couple conversations I can recall.

Fellowship Coffee September 2016

At our church, coffee is served in the Fellowship Hall before church service on Sunday morning. This Sunday morning Leone and I arrived about a half hour before the church service and I joined the folks having a cup and a donut. An elderly widow I have known for at least three decades said to me, "Nice shirt." "Well, you gotta get something new once in a while, I guess," I replied. "Your wife been shopping again?" another lady asked. "I just needed some new socks," I told her, trying to explain. "And you came out with a new shirt," somebody else said. About a half dozen church ladies sitting around the table smiled and chuckled knowingly.

One morning before church began, I was chatting with Don Konken and Paul Severtson in the hall. Our minister stopped by to say good morning and then he said something about marriage counseling. The rest of the conversation went something like this...

"You think we need marriage counseling?" he was asked.
"No, I might." he said.
"Oh, oh, what did you do wrong?"

"I bought a tractor at an auction yesterday morning."
(The minister and his wife live on a small farm and his affection for old tractors is well known.)

"Did you need it?"

"Of course I needed it, or I wouldn't have bought it."

"How did that work for you when you got it home?"

"Well, it has been awfully quiet around there lately."

Small towns—you gotta love 'em

You just need to remember that in a small town, rank has no privilege regardless of who you are or what you do for a living, and you need to learn to hold your own sitting around the "table of wisdom and knowledge" at the local coffee shop. Some might say it is the Great Equalizer. ☺

Five days after Christmas, our good neighbors invited us over for afternoon coffee. When we arrived at their home, Mr. Good Neighbor said, "I am sure glad that you folks came over, we have all these leftovers that we gotta get used up."

I called a gentleman on a recent evening, who is known to frequent our local convenience store/gas station about the time of mid-afternoon coffee. He told me he had heard a man that goes to my church was in very bad health and wondered if I could confirm that. "You can't always rely on everything you hear at the coffee shop you know," he said. No! Really? Now there is a shocker.

A MIDSUMMER WEDDING

July 2015

It was a warm, sunny afternoon with a blue sky and puffy white clouds in mid-July when Diane and Christ pledged their hearts and souls to each other forever with Reverend Alan Broadwell officiating. Mind you, these two are not some starry eyed kids who don't know siccum about life, like Leone and I were when we got married. Oh no, this was not their first rodeo, as some might say. The different roads they traveled to find each other here in Brownsdale were long, and not all of them were paved.

Christ came from Wisconsin. It took him nine years to make it to Brownsdale to meet the woman who was going to become his bride. His journey took him through Texas, Colorado, Wyoming, Oklahoma, and New Mexico to name a few of the places he had been, building windfarms, before he finally arrived here.

Diane was born in Cañon City, Colorado, and I guess you could say she spent her whole life working her way toward Brownsdale. She arrived here about the same time the Langtry Café opened for business. She was the first waitress hired, has been a part of our community ever since, and is well liked by everyone who knows her.

And quite a wedding it was! This was a real down home, old fashioned affair. There were the handwritten invitations with a verse from Solomon 3:4 that says, "I have found the one whom my soul loves" that were personally delivered.

The wedding took place in Todd Park. The alter was an arch created from three wood ladders tied together and covered with vines. And straw bales for folks to sit on, for those who didn't heed the advice in the invitation to "bring a chair". The tackle box next to the guest book with handwritten letters that said C A R D S worked quite well for that purpose.

Then there was the hay rack with a buggy seat fastened to it, for the bride and groom to take a ride around the park later on. There was food aplenty to enjoy. It was just a perfect afternoon for folks to sit around and visit with people they knew but probably haven't seen in a while. Warm, but not too warm, with a nice breeze. The bride was just beaming throughout the whole thing and the groom looked like…well, like grooms usually look at these things, I guess you could say.

It is my understanding that Jan Ball and Libby Barnes were the matchmakers for this marriage, but you will have to get the details from them. I'm not going there.

Happy Trails Diane and Christ, and remember…

The trail is the thing, not the end of the trail. Travel too fast, and you miss all of what you are traveling for.
~Louis L'Amour

OLD-FASHIONED SUMMER
GARDEN PARTY

July 2014

Gene and Sally Gerhart hosted an old-fashioned summer garden party Saturday afternoon. The weather cooperated and it was…well, summery, the way we imagine a summer day should be.

There was live music, games to play, plenty of food to eat.

It was attended by neighbors, friends, fellow artists, and their entire family - some from as far away as Texas and Washington.

A chance for folks to get together for some good old-fashioned fellowship.

The delicious meat was prepared by son Greg and all the food was served by Diane, a popular waitress at the former Langtry Café.

THE LANGTRY CAFÉ

April 2011

At a recent meeting of the Langtry Café Early Morning Coffee Gang Discussion Group, the subject of wives came up. One of the members piped up and said, "My wife complains that I don't listen to her when she is talking to me. At least, I think that is what she said."

Waitress Diane, also known as Alamo Annie, happened to hear this remark. She put that guy down so fast, I thought I heard a thud. The Discussion Group meeting was adjourned after that.

Diane gets respect. One day, a fellow was fiddling with her apron strings trying to get her attention. He wanted more coffee. She turned on him with coffee pot in hand and said, "You're gonna be wearing this coffee if you don't quit that!" He quit.

When Diane gets excited, she talks fast. About ten words per second, sometimes gusting up to 50.

(I heard later that after this had been printed in the newspaper there were several wives in town wondering whose husband had been fiddling with Diane's apron strings.)

Smiles are to people as sunshine is to roses. ~Tom Black

PERMIT TO CARRY

March 2013

One morning a couple weeks ago Phil Hatten, a member in good standing of the Langtry Cafe Early Morning Coffee Bunch Discussion Group, was chatting with Steve Nagel, proprietor, over coffee. Steve mentioned that he would like to get his Permit to Carry, but couldn't find a class. Phil said he had the name of an instructor. Somewhere along the way, DuWayne Skov suggested that they could use his farm for the shooting part of the class. Steve decided that maybe the Langtry Cafe could sponsor a class if they could get enough people interested to bring in an instructor.

It helps to understand how things work in a small town. Some things just seem to evolve over a period of time, with several different ideas being thrown into the pot and stirred around. Many times nothing comes of these "jawboning sessions," but once in a while, a really interesting project develops. That seems to be what happened here.

Phil called the instructor, who said he had to have a guarantee of at least 10 students to hold a class. Steve and Phil talked it over and decided to grant the instructor that guarantee without being certain of how many people would show up.

Steve put a signup sheet for the class near the door. They had over 20 people sign up in a short time, all they had room for at one time. After that class, he put up another signup sheet for another class, which filled up very quickly.

In order to receive a Permit to Carry, Minnesota law requires a person to complete a course that includes four hours of classroom instruction covering the basics of handgun use, the legal aspects of handgun possession, concealed carry and use for the purpose of self-defense, and the restrictions on the use of deadly force.

The course also included an hour of range time, which was conducted at the Skov farm, to make sure the applicant can safely and competently handle a handgun and demonstrate an ability to fire it at a silhouette target.

The word seemed to spread fast. Steve said he had planned on placing an ad in the *Meadow Area News*, but before he got around to it he had 40 people, both men *and* women, who said they wanted to take the class. This is about all they can handle. The cafe provided a continental breakfast for all attendees. Steve also said he was going to give each person who attends a coupon for a free meal at a later time, if they are "packing." Then he added with a grin, "I might not hold them to that last part."

These classes continued for many months. At one time, the Langtry Café even offered a discount to customers who were openly "carrying" when they came to eat. This practice was eventually discontinued after it started receiving mixed reviews from the rest of the customers when too many guys came for breakfast packing a pistol.

Did I mention that Steve was always quite a promoter?

AN OLD WOMAN DIED LAST WEEK

July 2015

She was almost 90 and had a hard life by many standards. A child of the depression like so many of us were. Times were hard for almost everyone back then. The "Great Depression" as it was called, started in 1929 with a stock market crash and lasted for 10 years. At its peak 25% of the workers in this country were without a job. There was no safety net for people without jobs, no social security, no unemployment insurance. It was "root hog or die" as they used to say back then.

She lost her mom when she was eight years old, was raised by her dad and eventually a step mom came along to help raise her and her siblings. She grew up, married and had six children of her own. Tragedy struck again when her husband died suddenly at the age of 39. They were living on a farm at the time, and she was left with the challenging task of raising six children by herself. She did the best she could with a big garden, a few chickens for eggs and meat, and for many long years a string of low paying jobs to bring in some money for things like kids' clothes, school supplies, car repairs. Her children learned how to work at an early age, I can tell you! It wasn't easy but by pulling together, they all got raised and graduated from high school.

"Bloom where you are planted" would be a good description of her life. She was active in her church, not afraid to express her opinion, a good worker, honest and dependable. That she taught these values to her children was obvious at her funeral.

We went to her funeral to pay our last respects. The church sanctuary was filled to overflowing for this simple, very old woman. Chairs were set up in the fellowship hall to accommodate everyone.

All of her children and grandchildren were there. Many of them spoke about their memories of "mom" or "grandma", some with a tear in their eye. And yes, she had a "wild child", maybe two, I don't recall. But I couldn't help noticing, all of them were dressed properly for the occasion, no shorts, no jeans. And no large disfiguring tattoos or metal objects protruding from their lips or nose.

You had a hard life old woman, but you did good, Evie, you did good. May you rest in peace.

It's not what you gather, but what you scatter that tells what kind of life you have lived. ~Helen Walton

MEANDERING THOUGHTS

May 21, 2008

I can't sit on the front stoop these days and enjoy a morning cup of coffee. Mrs. Finch has decided that wreath on the wall makes a good place for her home, and she just doesn't like people sitting right underneath her home.

This morning I stepped out on our back deck with a cup of coffee to enjoy the beautiful spring day. I promptly received a scolding from Mrs. Oriole. I didn't understand the words, but I definitely understood the tone of her voice. I retreated into the house to my chair by the window.

Dec 4, 2008

Two days ago we had about two inches of snow. Yesterday, about midmorning, Leone noticed some fresh deer tracks that went across our back yard, about 10 feet away from the deck. The tracks had *not* been there at first light. They seemed to go from north to south and stopped at the base of the dirt hill south of our place, as near as I could tell.

Curious, I put on a jacket and went out to investigate. I followed the tracks to the bottom of the hill, and they just disappeared at that point! Did the deer jump all the way to the top of the hill? They didn't go left or right.

Very strange. A white tail deer cannot jump that high. If not a white tail, then what. I wondered...could it possibly have been a reindeer, maybe, out for sort of a test run? After all, 'tis the season.

A true story, I swear. ☺

January 20, 2009

At a family gathering recently, I saw my cousin Betty for the first time in about five years.

She came over to me, put her arms around me and gave me a great big hug. Then she kissed me on the cheek and whispered in my ear… "You're gettin' old, cuz."

January 22, 2009

Leone used to cut hair for all of the family, including mine, but got tired of it after all the children were raised and gone. So I had to find a barber. The barber that I have gone to for several years died suddenly, age 63.

Leone volunteered to cut my hair one time while I looked for another barber. I took her up on her offer. As I sat down in the chair, I explained to her that when I went to our local barber, we usually discussed a variety of subjects, ranging from local "news", the economy, politics, religion, etc., while he was cutting my hair. So I asked her what subject she would like to start on. She said, "Just shut up for now, I gotta concentrate."

December 3, 2014

At the bank Christmas open house I was chatting with a couple I have known for a long time. As more people came in I got up to bring another chair to add to the circle of people enjoying coffee, Christmas treats and conversation.

I sat it down next to the fellow I had been talking with and told him, "I brought this chair over here in case someone who doesn't know you wants to sit down." He stared at me, his wife laughed, and he said, "I came here for free food. If I wanted abuse I could have just stayed home."

That Time of Year

It is the month of March.
The sun is finally shining.
There is no wind for a change.
People are walking across the parking lot at the grocery store in their shirt sleeves.
Cars drive by with their window down.
The thermometer on my car says it is 27 degrees outside.
You just know you are in Minnesota!

The Deer Hunter November 2000

I was traveling north to meet my 3 sons for our annual deer hunt in northern Minnesota. Leone had cooked a large pot of soup for us to heat and eat at deer camp.

While driving I was trying to remember if I had forgotten anything. I seem to always forget something, sometimes several things. I *knew* it! I don't have any crackers to go with the soup. After I leave the freeway, I am on 2 lane roads that pass through several small towns. I will find a grocery store in one of those towns, right next to the highway. Usually you can find a parking place close to the door. In and out, fast.

I spot the store I am looking for. I get my crackers and head for the check out. Second person in line. Great! While I am waiting, a guy comes into the line behind me. He is alone and has one item, a spatula. He also had deer hunter written all over him. I said to him, "You did pretty good. Only forgot one item." He looked at me without smiling and replied, "This is my third stop, and I still have one more to go."

I went into town to pick up some supplies. The young woman who waited on me had half the hair on her head shaved off, and the other half hung down to her shoulder. She also had four large white rings impaled on her low lip. I struggled not to laugh when I saw her. I described her to Leone when I got home and asked her, "What are these young people thinking to disfigure themselves in such a manner?" She shrugged and said, "I don't know." Then added, "Maybe it is some new form of birth control."

Small towns...

AKKERMAN MANUFACTURING
CELEBRATES 40 YEARS IN BUSINESS

July 2013

Just a little ways west of Brownsdale, tucked back in the woods, is a company internationally recognized as a leader in their industry. I am sure that many people who drive by and see the sign, Akkerman, wonder what they do. Akkerman's builds underground tunneling machines.

In 1954, Brownsdale resident Don Akkerman started a utility contracting business. They installed utilities underground the old fashioned way, by digging a trench. Don's wife Marlys ran the office and kept the books. They were a team. By 1963 Don saw a need for an underground boring machine. Don and his talented and mechanically-inclined employee, Don (Red) Lowe, built the first underground tunneling machine for the installation of 44" outside diameter concrete pipe.

After that, they built a 51" machine, followed by a 58" machine. These machines were all operated with a person inside. In the beginning, the machines were used by Akkerman Construction installing underground piping. In 1973 Akkerman Manufacturing was launched, in the business of making these machines and selling them to other construction companies. Akkerman Manufacturing started out in a garage that housed all facets of the business. As the business grew, expansions were made and today the plant and engineering spaces are housed in a 65,000 square foot building. The newest building is the corporate office, a state of the art 5,200 square foot building.

Over the years they have added many improvements, and variations of the original machine. They now offer both a manually operated machine and one that is completely remotely controlled by an operator on the surface. Akkerman's is still the only North American microtunneling equipment manufacturer. Akkerman and its equipment has been recognized for many awards and achievements throughout the years. In addition, Maynard Akkerman was honored for his service to the industry when named Trenchless Technology person of the year in 2008. In 2010

Akkerman was recognized for exemplary safety standards in its workplace by the Minnesota Safety and Health Achievement Recognition Program.

Akkerman's sold the first machine internationally in 1975, in Brazil. At the present time, they have machines in South America, Mexico, Australia, England and New Zealand to name a few. Now, sales to foreign entities accounts for 40% of Akkerman's sales.

Some of the more unusual jobs that used Akkerman equipment:

> Boring tunnels under the runways and taxiways while planes were arriving and departing, at airports in Chicago, Detroit, Denver and Los Angeles, to name a few.

> Los Angeles needed to dig a deeper ship channel to provide for heavier container ships. There were several utility lines that needed to be placed deeper before this could be done. Akkerman equipment was used to bore a tunnel under the bay for 800 feet.

> A more recent and challenging job was to tunnel under Miami Bay for 1200 feet to install a six foot diameter pipe for service to an island settlement where the rich and famous have homes. This was done 90 feet below the surface, completely by remote control.

Akkerman's employees 60 people at the present time, including five sales people. Rob Lorenzen, of Grand Meadow, is the only salesman that works out of corporate headquarters in Brownsdale. He is responsible for sales to the central U.S. and most of Canada.

The company has several employees with 20+ years of experience. They encourage employees to grow and be all they can be.

A quality product backed by good service has been a major factor in their success. Since the very beginning, whenever, wherever, they have sold one of their machines someone goes along with it. They make sure the machine is operating correctly and to teach the people who bought it how to run it. In the beginning Red Lowe was *the* man who went out with every machine. Today, the company has five technicians they can send out with a delivery. After that, there is a technician available by phone, any time a customer has a problem.

Some of these type of machines are built in Germany and Japan. The problem is getting parts if you break down. Akkerman maintains an inventory of parts for its machines that can be shipped to any place in the U.S. overnight. That is an important consideration for a contractor who may be on a job site with a full crew that must be paid and fed, working or not.

Akkerman's is owned by Maynard Akkerman and his wife Robin. Maynard started working with the company as a very young man and has learned the business from the ground up, or as some might say, the underground up. When Don retired in 1987, Maynard was named President of the company. I knew his dad Don, and I think that anyone else who remembers Don will agree with me. If Don didn't think Maynard could handle the job, he wouldn't have gotten it. Maynard has successfully steered the company through some difficult and challenging times since 1987.

Robin was more active in the early years, but as the children grew and required more of her time, she relinquished many of her duties at the company. She presently holds the title of Corporate Secretary.

Maynard shared with me an experience early on with a job in Canada using their new underground boring machine. Maynard and Robin's second child was two weeks old when he left. He was gone for six weeks. It was January. When he came home, finally, Robin said something to the effect that if it wasn't for the Grace of God and her parents, they probably wouldn't still be married.

Maynard and Robin have three sons. I have a strong feeling that when Maynard gets ready to call it quits, there will be a third generation Akkerman running the company.

FOSSTON MOTEL

November 2006

The big electric sign at the edge of the interstate, with the flashing electric letters, urges people to stop here.

CLEAN ROOMS

LOW RATES

EXIT NOW

This is not your usual Holiday Inn or Courtyard by Marriott.

No happy hour.

No continental breakfast.

Just clean rooms, low rates and an establishment run by three members of a somewhat dysfunctional "family" who love what they are doing.

Major credit cards, cash, personal checks and promises of future payment have all been accepted at this establishment, at one time or another.

It is old as motels go, I suppose. Getting a little run down around the edges, outdated perhaps, but well maintained. A horseshoe shaped affair with all rooms opening onto the parking lot in the middle, and everyone has to drive past the office to get in or get out.

Road Warriors - those well dressed, well-manicured, well educated young men and women, who fan out across the country every Monday morning for a week of trying to sell something to somebody - don't overnight here.

Herm is the patriarch of the family. Herm is in his late 60's with his second pacemaker. Herm almost always takes the night shift as desk clerk. He has been in some business or other for most of his life. Mostly just getting by, but always his own boss, not taking orders from anyone, and always treating everyone fairly.

Herm's wife came down with cancer after they bought this place. He took care of her until the end, even after she had to be in a wheel chair. Right there in the living quarters in the office of the motel.

The motel is the love of his life now, that and the people who help him run it and those who stay here. This place gives real meaning to the statement that "you are a stranger here only once."

Ruby is Herm's sister. She came here to help out with the cleaning and laundry, "for a while" 15 years ago. She drives 50 miles every day to work and is still here. Ruby's age is probably somewhere north of 60. She is still slim and erect, dependable and independent. Always a friendly smile. She will do anything to help you and make your stay more comfortable. She knows her job well, and does it her way. Don't try to tell her how to do her job, and don't make her mad. People foolish enough to have done either usually try to avoid doing it again. Except Ike.

Ike has worked for Herm in one business or another for about as long as anyone can remember. Ike is a middle-aged teenager. Friendly, helpful,  outgoing, always a smile, not a care in the world, unreliable, (totally unreliable, Ruby would say), those are some of the words that various people have used to describe Ike.

Ike likes to decorate the place. He decorates it for Halloween, Christmas, Easter, maybe even the 4th of July. "It makes the place seem real homey like," Ike says.

When Herm is really upset with Ike, Herm will tell you that the *only* reason that Ike is still here is because he can fix *anything*! Like the time that the big electric sign went off, in the winter. Herm called the company that had installed it. They came two different times before telling Herm they couldn't figure out why it wasn't working.

The sign not working was really hurting business. In Minnesota, it gets dark early in the winter. That big electric sign caught people's attention, if they were needing a place to spend the night. And the flashing words, CLEAN ROOMS, LOW RATES, EXIT NOW, pulled them in off the interstate.

Ike took his ladder and climbed up the sign at night to study the sign, and the bulbs. He did this for three nights before he figured it out. A small fuse in the line between two bulbs was the problem. Ike almost always has a furnace and an air conditioner or two disassembled in his small shop. No formal training, just a knack for fixing things.

Ruby and Ike do get into some pretty good quarrels sometimes. Herm got tired of it a couple years back. He told them he was selling the place and they would each get a third. "Good," said Ruby and Ike. A couple weeks later, the real estate agent said he had a buyer for a lot of money. Ruby and Ike came to Herm and said, "We don't want you to sell the place."

Herm got out of the deal somehow. Life goes on.

Ruby still cleans.

Ike still fixes.

Herm still runs the office.

About 4:30 pm in the winter months, later in the summer, people start stopping by.

A bell on the door announces someone coming in. Everyone gets a warm greeting and a smile from Herm. "Hi, how are ya? What can I do for you?"

There are new people to meet and maybe tonight, some old customers will drop in again.

And there are new experiences, as yet unknown, to experience.

Another night in the motel business has begun….

HUNTER-GATHERERS

December 2011

A hunter-gatherer or forage society is one in which most or all food is obtained from wild plants and animals, in contrast to agricultural societies which rely mainly on domesticated species. Hunting and gathering was the ancestral subsistence mode of Homo, and all modern humans were hunter-gatherers until around 10,000 years ago. Following the invention of agriculture, hunter-gatherers have been displaced by farming or pastoralist groups in most parts of the world. Only a few contemporary societies are classified as hunter-gatherers, and many supplement, sometimes extensively, their foraging activity with farming and/or keeping animals.

The last study from State Farm Insurance indicated that Minnesota was the 10th most likely state for drivers to hit a deer. Nationally, one in 183 vehicles will collide with a deer in any given year. The number of deer-vehicle collisions puts Minnesota in the risk category. Statewide deer-vehicle collisions in 2010 are on track with recent years. More than 1,900 collisions have been reported so far across the state, compared with more than 2,600 last year.

During the past five years, 20 of 24 deaths related to deer-vehicle collisions in Minnesota were motorcycle drivers, as were 107 of the 132 serious injuries. Nearly a quarter of the deer killed by cars in Minnesota each year meet their demise in the metro area, with Hennepin County leading the way with nearly 1,000 crashes during the past five years.

We have a couple older fellows in our area who could be described as modern day hunter-gatherers. They are avid hunters and children of the Depression. They hate to see food wasted, especially when they know folks in need. Somehow they started to pick up fresh road killed deer in the cold months that were in good condition. They process it themselves, even though this is a lot of hard work.

Because they have all the venison they need from their own hunting, I have learned (not from them, they don't talk about it or who it is given to) that venison from their foraging is distributed to local people who could use more meat in their diet.

It is nice to know that there are still thoughtful, caring hunter-gatherers like this in our community, who use their skills and talents helping others.

To every man there comes in his lifetime that special moment when he is figuratively tapped on the shoulder and offered that chance to do a very special thing, unique to him and fitted to his talents. ~Winston Churchill

LONG TIME LOCAL INSURANCE AGENT, JOY OUDEKIRK, RETIRES

September 2013

Joy started her career in insurance sales when she accepted a position in 1970 as secretary for the insurance agency then owned and operated by the 1st American State Bank of Brownsdale. She continued in that position, gradually acquiring all her insurance licenses until the agency was sold in 1978. She then became the agent for the new owners. When the bank was sold in 1998, the agency moved to its current location on Main Street.

I had the pleasure of working with her in those early years. She was very detail oriented. When things got busy for me, I knew I could place an application for insurance on her desk, feeling confident that everything was filled in properly before she would forward it to the company. She dotted all of my i's and crossed all of my t's for me.

Joy has seen many changes in the insurance industry, since she started 43 years ago. When she first started, all applications were filled in manually on a paper form. There was a printed form for every change made to a policy. She liked that, as she feels that good documentation is very important and it is more challenging to keep track of everything in this computerized world.

When asked about long term clients, she said that some of her clients now are third and fourth generation members of the same family. She has known so many of her clients for so long. One of the reasons it has been hard for her to retire is that she feels that all of her clients are like one big family, much more than just a business relationship. She has always enjoyed her work,  but there just comes a time when you have to make a decision, and she felt like the time for her to hang it up is now.

Several years ago she organized a defensive driving class in Brownsdale. It is held in the spring, usually before farmers get busy in the field. She keeps track of the people who have taken the class and notifies them when they are due to take another class. One of her other activities is to hold a meeting for farmers in late winter to go over all the annual changes to crop insurance policies.

I asked her if she could tell me about memorable experiences she has had during her years in the insurance business. After thinking awhile, this is what she told me.

In 1998 we had a bad storm with straight line winds that produced about 150 claims for her office. One of her insurance companies in southern Iowa sent their office staff up to Brownsdale to assist in filling out claim forms.

Crop insurance is a large part of her business. Because of our wet spring, many farmers were unable to get their crops planted. This is a covered loss under the multi-peril insurance. She held a meeting in her office for all concerned farmers, and brought in a couple insurance company representatives to answer questions. Following that was a great deal of reporting to be done, coordinating the activity of claims adjusters meeting with customers, etc. Things were pretty hectic for a while.

There were other challenging times that she couldn't recall right away.

But the one incident that will stand out in her mind forever happened in August of 2010. 08-09-10 to be exact. The day started out pretty much like any other day. Going through the mail, answering phone calls, talking with clients.

In the afternoon she made a visit to the John Schieck farm to measure some buildings for his farm insurance policy. They were at it a long time, and were almost done when a car drove in. John said he needed to talk to this person, could she please wait. She did, for about 10 minutes.

By the time she got back to her office, it was mid-afternoon August hot! She was thirsty and decided that a bottle of soda sounded good.

She went into the office, put her clip board on her desk, and walked over to the convenience store/gas station for her soda. As she was leaving, Gene Gerhart stopped her with a question. While they were standing by the door talking, there was a loud crash in the direction of her office. A loaded gravel truck had veered off the highway, drove over the front of Joy's car, crashed through the window, demolished her desk and filing cabinets behind the desk, and then came to a halt after striking a wall with enough force to cause serious structural damage to the building.

Investigation of the accident determined that the driver of the truck was dead at the wheel before striking the building. Cause of death was believed to be most likely a heart attack. Here is where it starts to get interesting. The insurance company for the truck denied coverage for the losses. The driver of the truck was not in control of the truck at the time of the crash, therefore it wasn't the truck's fault. This comes under one of the exclusions that is in all policies for "Acts of God". (Read the fine print in your policy, it is there.) I told Joy that it has always been a comfort to me to know that insurance companies believe in God. They must, otherwise they wouldn't list His activities as an exclusion in their policies.

Joy told me that afterwards, she thought a lot about the sequence of events that afternoon. What if she hadn't been delayed for about 10 minutes at the Schieck farm? What if Gene hadn't stopped her at the store with a question? Where would she have been when the truck struck her office? More "Acts of God"? Maybe. You decide. Joy tells Gene he saved her life that day and she tries to buy him coffee on that day each year to commemorate the event.

Joy has had a long and interesting career. Now she wants to focus more on her family, and lives on a farm near

Brownsdale with her husband Darrell. They have four children. Two of her children, Larry and Curtis, have a farming partnership that was started shortly after they left school many years ago. Joy tells me that Darrell is over to their shop every day, fixing on something, driving a load of grain to market, or working on something around the farm. Daughter Pamela is a 911 dispatcher and trainer in Stillwater and son Chris is a homebuilder in the Mantorville area. Joy and Darrell also have seven grandchildren and two step grandchildren.

Family and friends plan a retirement party for Joy for the afternoon of September 29 at the Brownsdale school.

Finally, Joy told me, with misty eyes, that she has so many good memories she was thinking about as she locked the office door for the last time, it was a long drive home. "How far is it?" I asked. "Eight miles." Joy replied.

Enjoy your retirement Joy. You have earned it.

PARAGLIDER PILOT MAKES
LANDING NEAR BROWNSDALE

August 2013

As I was returning to my home on the west side of Brownsdale Friday afternoon, I caught just a glimpse of what looked like a parachute coming down. It looked like it was coming down just to the west of the Akkerman Manufacturing location. Intrigued, I drove west around the bend to see what I could see.

There in the ditch on the west side of the road, very close to the high voltage transmission lines that run alongside that road, stood a man in a flight suit, helmet and all, with a parachute on the ground beside him. Where in the world did he come from? How did he get there? He said his name is Steve Markusen, age 59, from Minneapolis and that he is a paraglider pilot. He and some friends have found a minimum maintenance gravel road southwest of Sargeant and have been using it to launch their flights. He said it is really hard to find a quiet road without any utility lines running alongside or across the road. How they found this one is a story in itself.

These pilots spread their 'chute across the road, wait until wind seems right, then quickly lift their 'chute into the air and a tow truck with a very long cable pulls them into the air. Sometimes it is a jump start and sometimes it is about a 50 yard dash to get airborne. And sometimes they "get dirted". That is not a good thing. Once these bold airmen reach a certain altitude while being towed, they depend on finding thermals to extend their flight as long as possible.

A thermal is a rising column of warm air. They are created by the uneven heating of the earth's surface by the sun. A plowed field, a sand pit, a patch of woods, concrete or blacktop surfaces, all are good sources of thermals. Around here, confinement livestock buildings create their own kind of thermals from the methane gas rising out of them, according to paraglider pilot Steve, and you can get a really good lift from them!

Steve told me that he released the tow cable when he reached 2,000 feet of altitude after about a two mile tow.

He attained an altitude of 5,000 feet, gradually finding thermals and riding them as high as he could before starting to glide down looking for another thermal. As he went over Akkerman's he knew he was coming down as he had lost all lift. He spotted the high voltage transmission lines and cleared them. Barely, I thought, from where I saw him. Then he made a turn back to the north and landed in the nicely mowed ditch between the field and transmission lines. He made it sound so easy. He said he has landed on a two foot square target sometimes, just for practice. I don't think there can be more than 50 feet between the field and those high voltage transmission lines. That would be waaay too close for comfort for me.

He has been doing this for three years, has made 300 flights, the shortest about two minutes and the longest was 2½ hours, traveling 30 miles in that time. I asked him if he has had any "interesting" encounters with airplanes and this is what he told me. "I did have a plane fly below and to the front of me one time, between me and the tow rope. I think he saw me but am not sure if he saw the tow rope."

Steve asked if I would mind giving him a ride back to their makeshift runway on a gravel road. They have a chase car, but that could go pick up one of the other pilots if I would give him a ride. I was glad to do this to get a chance to see their setup.

I met two of the other pilots who were getting ready for a flight. One of them was an instructor in this unusual sport, a fellow from Texas who lives in a large 5th wheel trailer. He and his wife are what RVers call "full timers". They have crisscrossed the country for more than 20 years this way. There is a national association of paragliders so he just looks up a group wherever he happens to be when he gets the urge to fly. Unfortunately, he "got dirted" twice today.

It happened the second time while I was there. The winds were very light and variable. He was only a few feet off the ground when the wind shifted, partially collapsing his 'chute and it looked like he was dragged on the road a short distance before ending up in the ditch. The fourth pilot was still in the air. The last time they had heard from him he was somewhere southwest of Austin. He had been in the air for two hours when we were talking. Steve said he was the best pilot in their group. He is very good at finding thermals.

The state record for distance traveled by paraglider in Minnesota is 96 miles. The world record is 475 miles. For more information on this interesting hobby, check out the web site of the U.S. Hang Gliding and Paragliding Assn at www.ushpa.org.

When everything seems to be going against you, remember that the airplane takes off against the wind, not with it. ~Henry Ford

TRUE GRIT

October 2013

In my dictionary, among the definitions of "grit" are: firmness of character; endurance; courage.

In 1969 a movie came out titled *True Grit* starring John Wayne. It was about a one-eyed U.S. Marshal who exhibited all of the above qualities.

In the modern, highly electronic, instant communication society that we live in today, we seldom have the opportunity or the need to "test ourselves" to find out just how much "grit" we have inside us.

I would like to tell you a story about a modern day woman here in Brownsdale, Shirley Meier. I think this story is a shining example of real "True Grit" and should be an inspiration to everyone to remember the old adage, "Never Quit."

I had to talk long and hard to tell this story. Shirley is a quiet, private person. I tried to impress on her what a wonderful thing she could do by letting me tell her story. Who knows what person reading about her will be inspired by reading about her experience.

Perhaps someone greatly discouraged with a serious health problem, family problem, or financial problem will read this story and decide, if she can do that, I can certainly deal with my problem! How many people might be inspired to accomplish who knows what great achievements in their life by reading this story?

 Shirley lives in a century-old rural home on the edge of Brownsdale. She returned home from a shopping trip to town late one afternoon, about 5:30 pm. After depositing her groceries on the kitchen table, she went to the basement to get a rug, and in the basement she tripped and fell, striking her head on the basement floor. The fall caused her to break her hip.

Her first thought was, "I'm not sleeping down here on the floor tonight," and dragged herself over to the stairway.

In a choking voice, she told me, "I looked up those stairs and I prayed, *God, help me. I know I can do this.*"

Somehow, with a broken hip, at 86 years of age, she dragged herself up the stairs into the entry. Then she had to maneuver a turn and two more steps into the kitchen to where she thought the phone was on its charger on the wall.

It wasn't.

She dragged herself through the dining room, then through the living room, into the bedroom to get the other phone, which was dead because it was off its charger. She then dragged herself back to the dining room to an outside door that faces the back patio, where neighbors sometimes sit in the evening. Somehow, she pulled herself up to unlock the door and get it open. There were no neighbors on the back patio this evening.

She decided the only other option was to drag herself back to the kitchen and out the back door to her vehicle in the driveway, where she had left her purse (with her cell phone inside) in her vehicle.

As she was crawling past the table, she decided to prop herself up high enough on a chair to see if the phone could possibly be on the table. It was!

Her complete focus during this time was on finding the phone, and not thinking about pain, she said.

She called her daughter who had just driven to Minneapolis, and her daughter told her to call for help. After calling a fireman she knew on the rescue squad, he rounded up the rest of the team and they came to her assistance, convincing her she needed an ambulance.

Just then her son called to tell her an ambulance was on the way.

After arriving at the hospital, she declined any morphine or other pain killers, and said she wasn't feeling any pain. About 11 pm she finally gave in and agreed to accept some low-strength pain medication.

The next day she woke up with a full hip replacement.

After a short stay in the hospital, she went to Koda in Owatonna for recovery and physical therapy. In the second week after her surgery she was walking by herself without the aid of a walker or cane. Physical therapists were amazed and stated that it was one of the most incredibly fast recoveries they had witnessed. Due, no doubt, to her strength and determination. Five-and-a-half weeks after surgery she was back home.

When would have been the next time someone might have come to see her and, not getting an answer when they knocked on the door, might have opened the door and gone inside looking for her? She could have died in that basement.

People trying to call her would assume she wasn't home.

"I never doubted that I could do it," she said. "In a time of crisis, no matter what it may be, you have to create a feeling that you can conquer anything. Have faith, be strong, have great resolve, and focus only on your goal or destination."

"Grit." That's what I would call it -- "True Grit."

Whether you believe you can do a thing or not, you are right.
~Henry Ford

WHAT CAN JUST ONE PERSON DO?

September 2012

A plaque next to a small rocket sits in a clearing just west of Brownsdale on "Akkerman's Corner". It tells an interesting story. It was erected in 1997 to commemorate the 40th anniversary of Mousenik II, so I believe many people living in Brownsdale today have no idea what it is about. I realized this after a few people asked me, "What is that thing?"

Well, here is what the plaque says:

Mousenik Rockets

On 5 Jan. 1957 at the Red Rock Proving Grounds, (we live in Red Rock Township) located ¼ mile north of this marker the Austin Rocket Society launched a 4' 10" rocket.

Mousenik II

The rocket carried a live mouse as a passenger. The launch received international attention and coverage including ABC-TV's David Brinkley, MN Senator Ed Thye and Captain Charles Woody of the DoD missile office, who were all here for the launch.

The Mousenik I rocket achieved an altitude of 1,642 feet and a velocity of 221 mph. In 1958 the Austin Rocket Society set an altitude record of 3,250 feet.

The Austin Rocket Society was founded in 1955 by Richard King, Leonard Paul Germer and Gary Solyst, and was directed by Pacelli high school teacher Sister Mary Duns Scotus. They launched 35 rockets in 125 attempts. They were persistent. The 1957 members included Calvin Aaby, James Budd, Gordon Cassidy, Phil Grunewald, Carl Harwood, Gary Hitzeman, Wally Jensen, Steve Johnson, Bob Maile and Robert Simon. (Some of you old timers will no doubt recognize many of these names as being from the Brownsdale area).

I have it on good authority that the mouse passenger did not survive "reentry".

While this is an interesting story in itself, worthy of being remembered, there is another story here that I would like to tell.

It is about "just one person". In fact, she was "just" an old lady. She was "just" a homemaker and mother most of her life. She "just" lived in a small town. Her name was Lola Prigge. Now I don't know how old Lola was when she began this project, but she was well past the time when she qualified to be a "senior citizen".

And this monument was Lola's idea.

She went to the city council to get permission. They told her it is not in the city limits. We can't help you.

She went to the County Courthouse with her request. Someone there told her you have to talk to the County Commissioners. She went to a committee meeting. "We have to talk with the county engineer and talk about it and vote on it," they said. She went to another monthly meeting. And another. Maybe they got tired of her persistence, (isn't there a story in the bible about that, involving a king and a woman?) but *finally* they said OK, but we have no funds available for that project. She was persistent.

She found out what it would cost to build the rocket and the plaque and install them. Then she started hitting the businesses in Brownsdale for donations to do her project. She got the money!

Then she tracked down some of the local boys involved in the project and talked them into coming back to Brownsdale from far flung locations for the dedication at our annual town celebration. Four of them showed up, Steve Johnson, Paul Germer, Richard King and Phil Grunewald.

Brownsdale City Clerk Theresa Booms searched through her stash of articles about Brownsdale to provide me with much information for this article. Many thanks to her for her help.

The next time you drive by that little rocket west of town....think about what one person with some grit and determination can do.

A side note to this story. The boys in the rocket club had a key to the school and spent many evenings, **unsupervised**, in the chemistry lab at the school, mixing up different formulas for their fuel, as well as building their rockets.

———————✦———————

Every great dream begins with a dreamer. Always remember, you have within you the strength, the patience and the passion to reach for the stars to change the world. ~Harriet Tubman

PERCHERON

June 2018

The Percheron horse originated in the Perche Province of France. It has been recognized as a distinctive breed since the 1600s. As to the ancestry of the horse, some say it started with mares captured from the Bretons sometime after 496 A.D, some say it may have started with Arabian stallions brought into the area by invading Muslims in the eight century.

Wherever this breed of horse came from, Doug and Lisa Harrington have been working to improve the breed for many years on their farm near LeRoy, MN. Doug started raising Percherons with his dad more than 30 years ago.

Doug grew up around LeRoy and Lisa is the daughter of Jerry and Deanna Macvey from Brownsdale, MN. Jerry asked me to ride along down to their farm to take some pictures of a horse and I am glad he did. A most interesting horse, and huge. I asked Jerry how much that thing weighed and he guessed it would be over a ton.

Doug and Lisa have mares that have taken prizes at state fairs in Minnesota, Iowa, Nebraska and Missouri. Doug showed me two colts recently born from these mares. He said a man from Indiana bought two of his colts last year after seeing them on the internet and asked for first chance on the colts from these two mares. So, they will be going to Indiana when they are old enough.

They also have a beautiful three-year-old stud named Oak Creek Ace that they plan to present at the World Percheron Congress taking place at the state fairgrounds in Des Moines, IA in October. I asked Doug, "Why now?"

"Because," he said, "this show is only held once every four years, and usually somewhere along the east coast. The horse is in perfect shape now. It is his time."

Ace will be leaving their farm within the next month. A young man near Bloomfield, IA specializes in getting horses ready, getting "fitted" they call it, for shows and sales, so Doug feels it is worth it to have him prepare Ace.

Good luck Doug and Lisa, and Ace.

THE TALE OF NELLIE CROES –
A WAR BRIDE

June 2017

What is a war bride? Perhaps some of you older folks know the answer, but how many of the current generation know? They are the wives of American servicemen who fought in foreign countries. I believe the majority of these marriages occurred during WWII and the Korean War, but the term originated during WWI. Perhaps more than 65,000 women became "War Brides" during that time. Congress passed the War Brides Act in 1945 to exclude these women from the immigration quotas from various countries.

After the war, several ships were outfitted to accommodate transporting these women and their children to the United States from Europe. The Red Cross played a large role in relocating these women, while their husbands were still serving in occupied countries.

This story is about war bride Nellie Croes. Nellie told me that she was born in Juvincourt, France, a town about the size of Brownsdale. It is located in the historical area of northern France, about 200 miles from Germany.

She was 14 years old in 1940 when the Nazis invaded France. A day came when the Mayor of their town told the citizens that the Germans are coming to take over the town. Everyone has one hour to pack up and evacuate the town. (What would you pack if you had one hour to leave your home, probably never to see it again?)

Nellie remembers jumping into a ditch for shelter from enemy planes strafing the road, killing many people. They were buried on the spot and the band of evacuees moved on. The family eventually reached Paris and stayed with an uncle in an overcrowded apartment for some time. When the Germans reached Paris the family moved to a small town out in the country.

Watching American fighter planes dueling with Germans in the sky overhead was a common sight for her. (What this means is that she was watching two men in flying machines trying to kill each other.)

An uncle of hers, active in the French Resistance Movement, was caught and executed without trial.

Food was always scarce and life very uncertain. In 1944 American GIs liberated her town and there was great celebration. Nellie met an American soldier at that time and he asked her to marry him. She said no. He kept writing to her even after he returned home to the U.S.

Finally in 1947, she gave in and said yes. She moved to Austin, MN as the wife of Victor Croes, chef for the Jay

Hormel family, and settled into the Hormel household in Austin. Incredibly, Jay's wife Germaine was a French war bride from WWI.

Nellie will be telling all about her interesting life story, what it was like living in war torn Europe and her many travels since she came to America, at a program at Our Savior Lutheran Church in Brownsdale on June 25 at 2:30 pm.

Come and Listen. Ask her questions. Everyone is welcome.

Refreshments will be served after the program.

A ship in harbor is safe, but that is not what ships are built for. ~John Shedd

DUSTOFF 61

November 2012

In this day and age, we do not have a military draft. It has not always been that way. Not too long ago every able bodied man age 18 and up was given the opportunity, or should we say the requirement, to serve in the military service of our great country.

Today I had the privilege of visiting with a gentleman who had some interesting stories to tell. He was a young man too, once upon a time. He said high school was easy for him, he didn't have to study hard to get good grades and besides, there were so many fun things to do.

After high school, he tried going to college but soon found the rules were different and his grades weren't good enough to keep him in school. He knew he would lose his deferment so he beat the draft by enlisting in the army in February 1968. He took his basic training in Fort Campbell, Kentucky. While there went through a battery of tests, both physical and mental, that the military loves to give a trainee. He learned that he qualified for the WOFT program, which he learned was an acronym for "Warrant Officer Flight Training". He thought that was better than walking so he signed up for it.

He was eventually assigned to fly a medical evacuation helicopter. The crew consisted of a pilot, copilot, crew chief and medic. Pilots loved their crew chief because he is the one that kept that bird in the air, made sure all the systems were functioning, patched up the bullet holes when they returned from a mission, etc.. And he flew every mission with them, unlike the civilian contractors back in training school who stayed on the ground, and may or may not have fixed something the pilot thought needed attention. He also received the same medical training that all medics did. So, with his 200 hours of flight training and his training as a medic, he arrived in Vietnam in July 1969.

After a short period of "In Country Orientation", he was assigned to an active medevac unit, the 283rd Medical Detachment in Pleiku, Central Highlands, South Vietnam. They had crews on call day and night. One unit was always ready to go at a moment's notice, a backup unit was housed within 100 yards, but could rest on cots while waiting for a call. Others were called up from the barracks as needed.

These medevac units were situated around the country so that a combat unit could usually get help within 20 minutes or so, if they had wounded. These helicopters could carry six American or about 12 Vietnamese soldiers, plus the crew. The ground unit wasn't always factual about the severity of a wound, if the wounded soldier was a friend or the amount of enemy fire at the time, if they needed to get some severely wounded people out ASAP. In the daytime, the pilot would ask the ground unit to pop smoke to mark the landing zone. The ground unit would then tell the pilot what color they popped. Unfortunately, the enemy monitored our radio channel so when asked for red smoke, the pilot might see two red smokes. Hopefully, they would call for a color that the enemy didn't have. At night, the landing zone would use a flashing strobe light as the enemy didn't have them. Remember this was in the days before GPS so navigation was by compass course and best guess as to distance.

I asked if the enemy respected the red cross on the nose and belly of his chopper. He smiled as he explained that pilots thought they used these red crosses as an aiming point. He also explained the ZAP Zone to me. This was the small arms fire zone from the ground to 1500 feet above the ground. Pilots soon learned to forget about the landing approach and take off from landing zones procedures that they were taught in training. They developed gut sucking techniques neither condoned or approved by the military or equipment manufacturer, but survival is a powerful instinct.

By now some of you may be wondering who I have been visiting with.

Michael Harte - Helicopter Pilot - Dustoff 61. Michael lives with his wife Katherine in Brownsdale, and together they own IBI Data, a very successful business and a major employer in Brownsdale.

Michael's unit designation was Dustoff which told other units that this was a medevac unit with a medic and a pilot trained as a medic. The number 61 told others Michael was the pilot.

While Michael was on his one year tour of duty in Vietnam he tallied up over 900 combat flying hours in daylight and darkness. Using some quick math, this calculates out to more than three missions per day while on duty.

In his first month "in country" his chopper was badly damaged as it was approaching an LZ (landing zone), by what they took to be a farmer waving, but he was reaching for his AK 47 on his back. They aborted the landing and limped to a nearby air force landing strip where they basically crash landed. Michael took a bullet in his left arm in that incident.

On another mission, he was approaching a very small LZ amongst some trees estimated to be 80-100 feet tall. He had two gunships accompanying him, one on each side, firing rockets as they approached to clear a path, as this was a very "hot LZ", which meant there was a fire fight going on down there as they approached. He was able to land with a very tight circling maneuver, load four wounded and took off again, all in about five seconds. But he lost part of his horizontal stabilizers on the tail, whether from gunfire or contact with tree branches was uncertain.

While on his one year tour of duty, he was shot down two more times, and crash landed once, at night, in a fog.

I have talked with another man I know who flew in Vietnam in the larger twin rotor helicopters called a Chinook. I asked if he had any comments about the medevac guys. He said, "Everybody who was in Vietnam was brave, but these medevac pilots were the bravest of the brave. Every time they went out, they had to know they were going to get shot at, and might not come back. They had to have nerves of steel."

By the age of 21, Michael was back in the states, still young in years, but oh so old in experience.

Men such as this have sacrificed much. Many died. Many live with physical and emotional wounds for the rest of their lives, so that we can enjoy the freedoms we have today. Freedom isn't free. It is my fondest wish that it will help everyone who reads this understand and appreciate the wonderful freedom we have, thanks to those men and women who have answered the call of duty down through the years.

Freedom is never more than one generation away from extinction. We didn't pass it to our children in the bloodstream. It must be fought for, protected, and handed on for them to do the same.
~Ronald Reagan

SOME CALLED IT 'NAM,
OTHERS CALLED IT HELL

November 2013

After you had been there a few months, it was hard to tell the difference between the two. I visited with a man who was there. He talked to me about monsoons with their incessant rains that last for three months and turned everything into a quagmire of mud. He talked to me about the heat and humidity, the hordes of mosquitoes, the flies, and the huge rats that would sneak into the bunker that was your home away from home, at night. They would eat the calluses off your feet, if they were exposed, while you were sleeping, and anything else they could find to eat in the bunker. He found a hole where they were sneaking into the bunker, and killed 15 of them in one night.

He talked about living on C-Rations for weeks at a time, with only a hot meal once or twice a week, and about drinking water from a streamside purification plant at the same time that other troops upstream were bathing and washing clothes. A purification plant does not remove soap from the water so everybody had a very, very bad, extended case of diarrhea. He lost 30 pounds while in 'Nam.

He also talked to me about the need to wear your helmet and flak jacket every day, because of the incoming artillery rounds, of pulling guard duty night after night on the perimeter of the camp, in darkness so black it was almost hard to see your hand in front of your face. And how, if you stared at something you thought you saw out there in that darkness long enough, it would seem to move. But you weren't allowed to fire at anything without permission from officer of the day or sergeant of the guard.

Is it any wonder that after living under these conditions for months that he admitted to me that he developed what he described as "an attitude problem"? The army tries to maintain discipline under all conditions, so each morning the men were ordered to "police up their area" (that is military talk for "cleaning up" your area). Usually the men would walk from one side to the other, picking up pop cans or other large items, but ignoring cigarette butts and such.

One morning a young, snotty Second Lieutenant ordered him to pick up a cigarette butt he had missed. The soldier told him if he wanted it picked up he could do it himself! For this he received an Article 15 for insubordination and it cost him a stripe.

There seemed to be a tone of satisfaction in his voice when he told me the end of that story was about a month later. That lieutenant and another lieutenant that had backed up the charge were caught in bed together and released from the Army for conduct unbecoming an officer, or something like that.

Richard "Dick" Spinler lives quietly, (most of the time) with his wife, Mary, here in Brownsdale. He has three children and several grandchildren, all living in nearby communities.

Dick enlisted in the Army at the age of 17, in 1968. He enlisted for three years so he could receive training in mechanical work and his choice of where to be stationed, which was Germany. He was sent to Fort Campbell, Kentucky for his basic training and then on to Fort Polk, Louisiana for mechanic training.

After that it was on to Germany, all going as planned. *But*, after about six months he received orders sending him to Vietnam (why are any veterans who may be reading this not surprised?). Somewhere in the fine print in the contract you sign when you enlist are the words, "subject to the needs of the service" or something like that.

After arriving in Vietnam in March 1970, Dick ended up in a place called Camp J.J. Carroll, as a member of Bravo

Battery, 2nd Battalion (175) 94th Artillery XXIV Corp, which had a history extending back to WWII. He was there until November of 1970. If you Google Camp J.J. Carroll, here is some of what you will read:

> This was one of the biggest and most famous of the DMZ combat bases. It was established to stop the North Korean Army, massed in the DMZ just a few miles away, from invading South Vietnam.

> It was a crowded plateau just east of the highlands, enclosed by mine fields and concertina wire. At the time Dick was their the camp was occupied by about 300 U.S soldiers with eight of the real big guns, long range 8" guns. Our big guns put Camp Carroll on the map, especially the maps of North Korean Army gunners. Most of the casualties sustained at Carroll were from incoming artillery, rockets and mortars, almost all of Russian manufacture. The base was also occupied by about the same number of South Vietnamese troops with smaller artillery pieces.

> The base had been sprayed with Agent Orange, was treeless and practically no vegetation. Just a red clay that turned to dust each time a big gun was fired, and thick red mud during the monsoons.

Dick spent nine months at Carroll, starting out as a loader on one of the big guns, (remember that fine print I mentioned earlier about "subject to the needs of the service"?). He said that the guns could fire a projectile that weighed 200 pounds a distance of 20 miles. When they would receive a request for a "fire mission" from some unit in their area of responsibility, needing some artillery support, they would sometimes fire as many as 100 rounds.

He thought they may have averaged about 250 rounds a day. He has trouble with his hearing today.

From loader, he worked his way up to the position of the number two man, who was responsible for loading the powder charge, inserting the primer and firing the gun. This was done by pulling sharply on a lanyard to snap the firing pin. One time something stuck and the gun wouldn't fire. He jerked again on the lanyard as hard as he could, so hard in fact that he broke his wrist. He didn't realize this for some time, thinking it would get better.

He got off the gun when someone learned that he could do carpenter work and there was quite a stack of plywood that needed to be assembled. After the lumber was used up, he became a truck driver, hauling water and ammunition for the guns, over a road that was checked every day for mines the enemy may have laid overnight.

Another interesting operation he was involved with was Operation Lam Son 719. It took place in February-March 1971. This was an offensive campaign to destroy the Ho Chi Minh trail that went through a corner of Laos. This was the main supply route from North Vietnam to their troops trying to conquer South Vietnam. It was to be conducted by South Vietnamese troops with logistical, air and artillery support from the U.S.. Our troops had no authority to enter Laos and they had been caught there a couple of times previously.

Dick was involved with the artillery support unit that set up almost on the border. The fighting was fierce but the operation collapsed in the face of overwhelming numbers and a skillful foe. It was a disaster for the South Vietnamese Army, decimating some of its best units.

Dick said that for several days, they had been receiving incoming artillery fire at their base, and around it. On the day they were planning on pulling out, the incoming artillery became intense. He said the louder the sound, the closer that shell is to you.

He had pulled his truck over to the big guns for crew to load their belongings. He started for his truck when an incoming round sounded very close, and he crouched down in front of his truck for protection. The next round hit the rear of his truck destroying it. He ran for his bunker, which was a hole in the ground covered with sheet steel. Shells were exploding everywhere. Several other men huddled inside with him, one of them had his foot blown off before he got there. They figured out that much of the firing from earlier days was to get the range on the camp so when the enemy was ready to attack, they could lay down an effective barrage.

Orders came to abandon the camp immediately. He had to leave behind about 20# of C4 explosives that he used to heat his C-Rations, about eight cartons of cigarettes, and a machine gun. Fortunately he survived.

He also spent some time in DaNang, other various fire bases and Camp Eagle at Hue. Somewhere along the way, he was hit in the leg by a piece of shrapnel, which earned him a Purple Heart, a medal given to soldiers wounded in battle. He finally went to sick bay about his wrist that was still bothering him. Almost a year since he hurt it, he learned that it was broken, had never healed, a small bone in the wrist had died, so it wouldn't ever heal.

He was sent back to the states immediately on a medevac flight without a chance to pack his personal belongings. He said he felt uncomfortable on the flight because so many of the men had such terrible wounds that a couple of them died on the flight. When he arrived in the states he was sent to Fort Sam Houston in Texas for medical treatment.

He served almost 16 months in Vietnam. He had extended his tour intending to stay until he was within five months of his discharge date, when the rule was, you could get an early discharge that way. He was sent home less than a month before he reached the five month period, so he was required to serve more time in the Army here in the states before he was discharged.

The saddest thing he remembers is what happened to a couple soldiers he had deployed to Vietnam with. They were about two weeks from their time to rotate back to the states. They were riding in a truck that was pulling their disabled self-propelled gun, and it was blown up by a land mine. Everybody was thrown out of the vehicle by  the force of the explosion, but these two ended up face down in a rice paddy. It was determined later that they had both drowned. Their arms and legs had been broken by the force of the explosion so they were unable to turn themselves over.

Dick said that he felt the infantry had it much worse than they did. He met men in Vietnam that he has kept contact with, and they still get together from time to time.

This was probably this country's most unpopular war, up to that time anyway. Protesters, who somehow managed to avoid the draft, were always out and about. Returning veterans were at worst, cursed, spat upon, called names, as if the war was their fault. At best, people ignored them. No parades celebrating their return, no hero's welcome, nothing. Sadly, many young people today don't even know what Vietnam is or was.

I read an article in a recent issue of my "American Legion Magazine" that talked of the physical hardships and emotional trauma suffered by the soldiers in Vietnam. The article asked the question, "Where do they find such men?"

Where indeed?

Patriotism is supporting your country all the time, and your government when it deserves it. ~Mark Twain

DEXTER'S WAR

November 2018

Veteran's Day is a national holiday held on November 11. It began as Armistice Day on November 11, 1919, the first anniversary of the end of WWI. It is a day set aside to remember the sacrifice all veterans, living or dead, have paid to protect and defend the freedoms we enjoy. I have heard it said, "All gave some, some gave all".

The Vietnam War is a good example. In total, 58,307 American men and women lost their lives in that horrible, useless war. If only our "leaders" who think it is necessary to go to war had to lead the charge, I just wonder how many wars we would have.

For many years, I have remembered hearing about three young men from the Dexter area who made the ultimate sacrifice. And I decided I wanted to learn who they were and write a story about them.

I must admit that this was a bit of a challenge. I told the editor of the *Meadow Area News,* Marceil Skifter, that I wanted to write about this but was having a hard time learning the names. She suggested I contact Eris Bakken in Dexter. Marceil told me that she may be 95 but she is still as sharp as a tack. I did and she is.

One of the men I was trying to get some info on was Leo Michael. Eris said she had never heard of any Michaels living in Dexter. She asked her brother. He never had heard of any Michaels either. Eris suggested I talk with Dexter City Clerk Natalie. I did. She had not heard of him either. Natalie sent me to Ray Tucker. Ray was familiar with three men from the Dexter area dying in Vietnam, but he gave me the name of another man who lived a few miles south of I-90 with an Elkton address. Now I had four men instead of three and I have a mystery inside my original story. Bunny trails!

I was talking with Marceil about my frustration. Everything I could find about Leo Michael indicated he grew up and is buried in Des Moines, IA. There is a small town in Iowa named Dexter. (Again, thanks to Iris.) I looked up the location of Dexter, IA and it is just a short distance west of Des Moines! I then became convinced that they had made a mistake on the Vietnam Wall Memorial. With 58,307 names carved in granite.

Marceil reached out to Sue Doocy, who does research at the Mower County Historical Society. She dug up an incredible amount of info and solved my mystery with a copy of a short death notice in the Austin Daily Herald from that era. It said Leo Michael was a marine who had died in Vietnam and that he had formerly lived with his sister and her husband, Wayne Ridengour, on a farm near Dexter! Mystery solved. Part of it anyway.

On a web site www.virtualwall.org I was able to learn that Leo's death was listed as "accidental homicide" in a battle in Quang Nam province. His job description is listed as "rifleman" (a very risky occupation). I asked another Vietnam vet, Don Konken, if that was army speak for something called friendly fire. He said it was. In this case I later learned that a fellow marine was crawling to change positions when his rifle discharged accidently, killing Leo instantly. He had served in the Marine Corps for eight years and was 26 years old. So sad.

Wayne Mees grew up on a farm near Dexter, went to school, loved to play basketball with a neighbor boy named Stanley Gilbert.

December 1966 was when Wayne arrived in 'Nam, job title listed as Infantryman. Just a little over three months later he was killed in action of multiple fragmentation wounds in Dinh Tuong Province. Age 20.

Danny Wilson grew up west of Elkton, just a few miles south of I-90 that borders Dexter. He loved farming and his family believed he would come back from the army and start farming with his dad. They already had 40 milk cows together and were planning on renting some land.

Danny arrived in Vietnam in July 1969. He was involved in three different campaigns. It looks like he was almost continually in combat offensives. The last one was a large scale push into Cambodia to drive Viet Cong out of a sanctuary area they had established. Danny died from hostile gunfire while operating as a machine gunner in a helicopter that crashed June 26, 1970. 21 years of age. A Future Farmer of America.

And the fourth member of this exclusive little group was a man named Stanley Gilbert. Stan loved basketball and football. Graduated from high school, went to carpentry class at the Vo-Tech in Austin to learn to build houses like both his grandads did. Stan got engaged. Then his draft notice came and he went off to serve his country like his dad did, as well as both grandfathers, leaving family and fiancée behind.

He arrived "in country" as they called it, on Jan 9, 1967. On October 17, his unit was ambushed while they were on a search and destroy mission. Stan carried an M-60 weapon. Part rifle, part machine gun I would say. The thing weighed 23 pounds plus the weight of a hundred round ammunition belt. And I would imagine you needed to carry at least two or three of them on your shoulder. I never knew Stan, but I know that it would take a *big man* to carry such a weapon around all day.

When the unit was ambushed, several men were wounded, including Stan. Though wounded, he moved to put himself between his comrades and the enemy to allow time for them to be evacuated. The usual practice was for the Viet

Cong to walk around and kill the wounded after a battle. They found his body three days later. Stan was awarded a Bronze Star posthumously for this action.

A fellow trooper, Dr. Chris Ronnau wrote about Stan in a book titled *Blood Trails*.

Go to the web site, Virtual Vietnam Veterans Wall of Faces, www.vvmf.org. As one contributor wrote, "We need not only to remember their names but also never forget their faces." Type in Stanley D. Gilbert, scroll down to Remembrances. Read them all if you wish but go to page two and read the posting by Bernadine Gilbert Lee titled "A Soldier's Story". Let me know if you can read it all without discovering a tear rolling down your cheek.

Below is an excerpt from that posting:

Two weeks later, Mom stood in the kitchen and glanced out the window. She watched as her son in his Army fatigues slowly walked down the drive. She saw him fade away and knew without doubt, a soldier's soul had come home.

I WILL MISS YOU, MY FRIEND

May 2019

I lost an old friend last week. He was 95 years old when he passed away, after living a very full life. He was a member of what has been described as "The Greatest Generation". These are the people who were born and grew up in the depression of the 1930's and became adults during WWII.

After Vern came home from the war he married the sweetheart he had left behind, as so many men had done. They settled into a farm they bought in Dexter Township, where they lived their lives together farming and raising three children.

I believe it was after all their children had grown up that he became involved with IBI Data. Vern was a master craftsman when it came to woodworking. I think he liked building porches as well as cabinets and a host of other things.

He remodeled the houses north of Brownsdale called Josie's House and Jessie's House, converted an old barn into a stable as well as many projects at IBI Data.

The love for this man was evident by all the stories told by family members at his funeral. He taught me to play a game he liked called Pente. It is played on a checker board using stones. What he didn't teach me is how to beat him in the game. I still liked playing it. He was still pretty sharp well into his 90's.

He was a well-respected farmer who cared well for his family, served his community by serving more than 30 years on the Dexter Township Board, and served his church, The First Baptist Church of Brownsdale, as a member and a Deacon of the church.

And he served his country also, as a pilot in WWII. He enlisted when he was 19 years old. After learning to fly in an open cockpit aircraft, for a month, he graduated to training in a twin engine aircraft. About four months after his 20th birthday, Vern and many others like him were considered "trained enough" and sent off to war.

Vern's war was flying a twin engine cargo carrying aircraft which was a military version of a DC-3. This was flying through the Himalayan Mountains on a route from Burma to China. He got there by flying as the co-pilot on a C-47. The route took them from Florida through Brazil, Cairo, India and then China. He spent Thanksgiving 1944 in Kung Ming China and then started flying trips hauling 50 gallon drums of gasoline as cargo. I would ask him about his experiences sometimes when we were playing Pente. You kind of had to drag it out of him. He told me one time that it was said that you could walk for 300 miles on aluminum along the route they flew.

Recently I Googled "The Hump WWII" and some of the things I learned include:

o "The Hump" was the nickname allied pilots gave the Himalayan foothills, as well as "Skyway To Hell" and "The Aluminum Trail".

o It was the Army Air Force's most dangerous airlift route, but it was the only way to supply Chinese forces as the Japanese controlled the land routes.

o It was incredibly dangerous to fly this route. The mountains caused jet stream winds of 100 mph and created dangerous weather at extreme altitudes. Sometimes pilots would be plodding along at ground speeds of 50 mph, fighting a headwind when they would get caught in an updraft lifting them quickly to 28,000 feet and then plummet them in a downdraft just as suddenly to 6,000 feet.

o If the pilots weren't fighting the ice storms or thunderstorms, there was always the danger of the Japanese prowling around looking for them.

o Customarily, in order to maximize the payload planes carried very little extra fuel beyond what they needed to get to their destination, leaving little margin for error.

o The pilots were mostly inexperienced flying anywhere, much less in extreme weather conditions in remote areas.

o   A full one third of the men flying this route died there.

o   Between 1942 and 1945 700 aircraft and their crews
    went down trying to cross The Hump. *500 aircraft and
    their crews are still missing!*

Vern did consent to giving an interview to someone
gathering info for a national archive about the stories of
WWII. These are some things I learned from reading that,
thanks to Michael Harte helping me find it.

Vern said they flew three days in a row and then were off
one day. He did this for 13 months before the war ended.
Because of the urgency of the mission there were very few
days that they didn't fly because of weather. From what I
have read elsewhere, the attitude seemed to be that they are
churning out new pilots and planes every day so the risk
was worth it.

When returning from a mission, they weren't allowed to
land if enemy bombers were in the area, which got a little
hairy sometimes because they were always low on fuel.
Several nights they spent in a slit trench because their
airstrip was being bombed or strafed by enemy planes. They
lived in shacks with smoke holes above the timberline.
Elevation at the airstrip was 7,000 feet! They ate the same
food as the Chinese - rice, bread and eggs, and did their
own cooking on a flat top stove in their shack.

The operations office had five gallon cans of deicing fluid
for fuel to heat the place when it was cold. He was at a
place called Changi when the war ended. He took a plane to
Casablanca, then a luxury liner back to the states and a train
home.

I never could understand how men that had such experiences could recalibrate to the peaceful, quiet life of a small town in the Midwest.

"Where did they find such men?" someone once asked.

Where indeed?

And I can't help but wonder if the need arises, could we find such men and women again to serve and protect our country?

Rest in peace, my friend. You have earned it.

It is in your moments of decision that your destiny is shaped.
~Anthony Robbins

A BRIEF HISTORY OF THE
ARTIFICIAL POPPY

November 2011

In the WWI battlefields of Belgium, poppies grew wild amid the ravaged landscape. How could such a pretty little flower grow wild while ‾surrounded by death and destruction? The overturned soils of battle enabled the poppy seeds to be covered, thus allowing them to grow and to forever serve as a reminder of the bloodshed during that and future wars.

The poppy movement was inspired by the poem "In Flanders Fields" written by Lieutenant Colonel John McCrae of the Canadian forces in 1915 before the United States entered WWI. Selling replicas of the original Flanders' poppy originated in some of the Allied countries immediately after the Armistice.

Each year around Memorial Day, Veterans of Foreign Wars members and American Legion Auxiliary volunteers distribute millions of bright red poppies in exchange for contributions to assist disabled and hospitalized veterans. The program provides multiple benefits to the veterans and to the community. The hospitalized veterans who make the flowers are able to earn a small wage, which helps to supplement their incomes and makes them feel more self-sufficient. The physical and mental activity provides many therapeutic benefits as well.

Donations are used exclusively to assist and support veterans and their families. The poppy also reminds the community of the past sacrifices and continuing needs of our veterans. The poppy has become a nationally known and recognized symbol of sacrifice and is worn to honor the men and women who served and died for their country in all wars.

Last week I happened to be in Austin when the ladies of the Veterans Auxiliary were out offering their poppies in exchange for a donation to this very worthy program. It was one of those chilly, windy days. The two ladies in front of Walmart looked like frozen popsicles. I asked why they weren't inside and was told Walmart doesn't allow that, but it is OK for them  to stand outside. As I continued my shopping I learned that Hy-Vee, Shopko and other stores allow these volunteers the shelter between their doors.

At least Walmart is better than the U.S. Post Office. I learned that the U.S. Post Office doesn't allow the Legion

Volunteers to even stand on the sidewalk outside the post office, BUT THE POST OFFICE IS CLOSED ON VETERAN'S DAY BECAUSE IT IS ONE OF THEIR LEGAL HOLIDAYS.

Let me see know if I can figure this out. The Post Office doesn't allow military veterans organizations to even stand on what they deem to be their property, but they close up and take the day off to observe Veteran's Day. No, that is too deep for me. Can anyone out there explain that one to me.......?

Oh, and if you are in Walmart some time, tell them thanks for supporting our troops, (as their numerous ads proclaim) but how about supporting our veterans also?

Personally, I think it is too bad that some of the people making the decision that it is necessary for our country to go to war, didn't have the opportunity "to walk in harm's way" for a while, leading our troops into battle in the service of our great country.

Only two things are infinite, the universe and human stupidity, and I'm not sure about the former. ~Albert Einstein

MEMORIAL DAY, SMALL TOWN STYLE

May 2017

The Civil War ended in 1865. It claimed more lives than any other war in American history. Fallen soldiers were buried in cities, small towns and hamlets across the land.

By the late 1860's, citizens in various towns and cities had begun holding springtime tributes to these fallen, decorating the graves with fresh flowers, having a small ceremony, saying a prayer or two. By 1868 a day in late May was designated as a National Day of Remembrance and it was called Decoration Day. It originally honored only those who had died in the Civil War and it was observed on May 30.

After WWI, it became Memorial Day to remember all soldiers who have sacrificed their lives to protect the many freedoms we enjoy today. And it gradually became a day to remember family members and friends who have passed away.

I believe it was in the mid 60's that Memorial Day became the last Monday in May, giving people a three day weekend to celebrate the beginning of summer.

This Memorial Day, I attended the ceremony at Greenwood Cemetery, just south of Brownsdale. I was heartened to see more than 60 people, young and old, in attendance. Many of the folks were walking around, stopping at a grave marker here and there, remembering something about a loved one who has passed away.

I heard Truman Olson telling Gaylord Tapp that Memorial Day always reminded him of his brother who had been killed during the Battle of the Bulge. (The Battle of the Bulge was a horrible battle in WWII. More than 19,000 Americans were killed during a week period, in the winter months of December and January. It was a turning point in the war.)

The Honor Guard from the Hayfield American Legion Club appeared at the appointed time, 20 strong. They formed up next to the bus they arrived in and marched into the cemetery and stopped where the ceremony was going to be held, standing at rest.

Opening remarks were given by Dave Haukom, Commander of the Hayfield American Legion. A prayer was offered by Reverend Prigge of Our Savior's Lutheran Church of Brownsdale.

The Honor Guard was then called to attention and fired three rounds from their rifles, a traditional military farewell to a fallen comrade. After that a bugler played "Taps", a haunting melody:

> *Day is done, gone the sun,*
> *From the lakes, from the hills, from the sky.*
> *Rest in peace soldier brave,*
> *God is nigh.*

Before the days of radios and telephones, soldiers were given orders by various bugle calls, and "Taps" originally meant "lights out", signaling the end of the day. Over time it became a final farewell to a fallen soldier and is commonly played at all military funerals.

Frank Moon ended the service by reading the Benediction. This was followed by Bonnie Nelson and her daughter Sharrie Garbisch taking turns reading the names of the 117 people buried at Greenwood who had seen military service.

On this Memorial Day I can't help but think of all the young lives that were cut short by war, defending our freedoms that we hold so dear. (And unfortunately, many people today take these freedoms for granted as their "right"). What could they have accomplished if they had been allowed to live out their lives?

Anybody who does not show respect for our flag is being disrespectful to the sacrifices made by these men and women.

Do what you can, where you are, with what you have.
~Theodore Roosevelt

The following story was written by our grandson Joseph Peterson. It is about an experience he had while serving in the Peace Corps in Africa. I thought it was so well written that I asked him if I could include it in this book and he gave me his permission.

JOE'S WAR

Posted on July 31, 2012 by peacecorpsjoe

They invaded the first night. It was an ambush, I was unprepared for the onslaught that occurred. It was a pitched and heated battle that raged all night. Who was this new enemy, what did they want, where did they come from and why are they attacking?

Respite came at dawn. The enemy had me on the ropes but for reasons I am only now beginning to understand, they withdrew. The light gave me time to assess the situation and fortify my defenses. They came again the second night but this time I was prepared and the line held. Again the third night and so on for the last two months.

The losses on both sides are high, the soldiers are tired and supplies are running low. Most nights I succeed in the holding the enemy at bay, but they are cunning and smart. They probe and exploit every weakness, every opportunity to slip behind my lines. Who is this enemy you ask? They come from the bush and know the land, they are ancient and have been here for millennia, they strike fear and terror into men. Countless books and movies have depicted them as the "thing" that comes in the night. You know them as...lizards.

I! HATE! LIZARDS!

Every night is a struggle to find new and innovative ways to keep them out of my room. I have spent the last two months shoving everything I can get my hands on into the walls to fill the holes in the walls. They are not large holes but they are big enough for the little geckoes to get in.

Just when I think I have completed my task, I find one of them on the wall. Once I have chased it out and found its entry point, PLUG! Everything from packaging material to the bags the laundry detergent comes in. The large, yellow headed "Push Up" (fill in your favorite explicative here) are the worst. I call them "Push Up" lizards because they run for a short distance and then stop and do pushups. They click, and when they get on the tin roof and sound off at all hours of the night, it is like trying to sleep inside a base drum during a rock concert. I am not kidding you, the tin roof and the echo in the concrete box I sleep in make it sound like a Black Cat firecracker is going off above my head.

What to do? Only thing I can do is chase them off the roof once they are up there, but that requires getting out of bed and throwing rolls of TP at the underside of the roof until they leave. My journey here was to teach, but I have found a new quest. I have found a new passion and a new hatred. I vow, right here and now to the whole world, that I will remove from this country every low down, rotten, stinking, yellow headed hell spawn that I can find. I bid you farewell, hopefully we will see each other again…

ONE TOUGH TRUCK
OR – OWNER TESTIMONIALS FORD MIGHT NOT TELL YOU

March 2011

My son–in-law Bob has a truck. It is an old truck. And it is one tough truck. It is a Ford F-150 4WD. It came off the assembly line in 1993.

The first owner was a logger, and he used it in his logging business in the back country of northern Minnesota. No highway miles there.

After Bob acquired the truck, in some sort of trade that I never did fully understand, he used it for work. Bob is a rodbuster, one of the toughest jobs in construction. For several years he has been involved in building windmills in the western states. Out there - Wyoming, Oklahoma, New Mexico, Texas - they like to build these windmill farms in isolated areas. Fewer "PR" problems that way, I guess. Not all of those roads are paved. Heck, some of the places he has gone, there wasn't even a road. He drove to the job site with other workers, loaded with supplies and equipment. There were times when he pulled loads way beyond the "maximum load range" that the Ford Motor Company recommended for this truck. But I think those are the primary reasons a fellow buys a truck. To work. Not to take their date to town, or pull a fancy boat like some of those ads you see on TV.

OK, so it got a little banged up along the way. And Bob is not sure of the actual number of miles on this truck. The odometer has not actually been, ahhh, in continuous service, shall we say, since the truck left the factory.

Something hard collided with the windshield, but fortunately it is on the passenger side so it doesn't obscure the drivers vision... much. And some of the paint on the front fender, that replaced the original one, almost matches the color of the rest of the truck.

A little, short stubby screw driver laying up on the dash works quite well to start the truck, since someone broke the key off in the ignition.

Good old reliable duct tape is doing a fine job of holding the steering wheel together, as you can see. I think that the seat and flooring are getting to look a little ragged, but Bob says they are good for a long time yet. You can only see through the floor boards in a couple of places. And the heater still works....kinda.

Both front and back bumpers are starting to waste away, and if you look closely, you can see that the tie wire picked up on a job site, is doing a good job of holding the side mirror on its bracket. And both doors still open... from the outside anyway.

The truck is back in northern Minnesota now. It will spend the rest of its days working in the woods again. In addition to construction work, Bob and Corrine have a large stand of maple tree on 100 acres situated waaay back in the woods and they produce maple syrup in the spring of the year. Bob has more than six miles of plastic tubing strung between the trees, numerous sap ladders and over a mile of plastic pipe used to move the sap from the woods to the processor. He will put in about

3,700 taps and if they have a good year, will produce over 1,000 gallons of maple syrup. The truck is used to haul material into the woods as Bob adds to his lines. It can bull its way through a lot of snow if it has to. It still starts readily enough with the makeshift key, in the worst of weather .

It is still one tough truck.

On a recent trip back from town to pick up supplies, I asked Bob is this truck was "street legal". He grinned and said, "Well, in these parts it is."

Well, that's my tough truck story.

What's yours?

SNOW PLOW MAN

January 2014

Last weekend we drove to Wisconsin to see our grandson Joe, home from Africa for a short visit and to be present for the baptism of our great-granddaughter.

The weather was cold and we battled a strong south wind with blowing and drifting snow for the entire journey. I was tempted to cancel the trip because of the weather, but knew I couldn't. It would be our only chance to see Joe and great-grandma was so looking forward to seeing our great-granddaughter again.

We arrived at our son's home about 3:00 pm. No one was there except Joe. His mom was still working, and so was his dad. In a way, that wasn't all bad. It gave us a good opportunity to spend some quality time with Joe, and catch up on his experiences.

In our lives, we have learned to stay flexible. The plan was that our son Steve was going to prepare some of his delicious ribs for our supper. But, that changed. Steve operates a lawn care business in the warm weather months and is a part time snow plow driver for the township in the winter months.

Normally, there are two older gentlemen, Merle and Harry, who are the regular snowplow operators. Merle celebrated his 75th birthday some time ago. For Harry, the 60's will soon be just a memory. Unfortunately Harry suffered an injury while standing on a bracket in the engine compartment (the hood on these large trucks open from the back) while trying to fix the windshield wiper on his snowplow. He slipped and ended up dangling upside down on the outside of the truck, with his foot caught in the bracket in the engine compartment.

Now, in the old days, on an isolated township road in mid-winter, he would have just "hung out" like that until someone happened to come along. But, we live in the modern age of high technology so he got out his cell phone, dialed 911 and summoned help. He will be on the disabled list for the rest of the winter.

So, part time snow plow guy is now getting a whole lot more work than he bargained for. His area has had a lot of snow and wind, so the snow plow guys have been out a lot.

Did I mention that Steve lives in the beautiful rolling hill country of Wisconsin? It is not all flat like it is around southern Minnesota, with most of the roads laid out in nice neat one mile squares. Where Steve lives, it seem like you are either going up a hill or around a curve, and sometimes you are doing both at the same time. And, *and,* these are narrow township roads, not the nice wide roads like the state and county guys get to plow.

Because of the blowing and drifting snow that day, Steve had been called out for snow plow duty. The east-west roads were drifting over and icing up. He stopped by the house about 4 pm, asked Leone if she would like to fix supper, told her what to fix and where it was. He asked me how I would like to ride in a snow plow because it was going to be awhile before he finished his work. What a great opportunity to spend some time with my son and see what he does.

I did inquire about any rules regarding passengers in the snow plow, just out of idle curiosity. I think at that point only an armed police officer standing in from of the door would have prevented me from going along. Steve said, "I asked Merle about that one time, because he takes his wife along sometimes. She gets bored sitting at home alone." His response was something to the effect that if anybody didn't like it, *they* could get out on Christmas morning and plow snow and *he* would sit home by the fire with his wife. 'Nuff said.

I climbed the three steps up into the cab. These trucks are a lot taller than they look. It is an interesting perspective from inside the truck because you sit up so high. You are looking down at everything. With those narrow twisty roads, and that great big truck with a plow on the front and a seven foot wing on the right side that he raises and lowers as needed, it is a wonder that he doesn't take out a sign or a mail box now and then, but I didn't see him hit a single one - although he gets really close to them sometimes! The turning radius of this truck is amazing. I couldn't believe the tight little area that he could turn that great big thing around in. When loaded with gravel for sanding the whole rig weighs in at 44,000 pounds!

And then there are the sounds. I was surprised at the noise level. When he drops the blade to clear the road and lowers the "wing" to push the snow further away from the road there is quite a din and clatter with the plow dragging on the road, the wing banging against hard crusted snow, and metal braces and brackets striking against one another, in addition to the growl of that big engine and the rattling of the tire chains on the road.

Eventually you realize that your feet are getting cold, but your face feels flushed. That is because the heater is going full blast, but all of it is going into the defroster. The wiper blades run continuously as fast as they will go. It is important to try to keep the windshield as clear as possible. This is because when the wind is from the right side of the truck and he hits a large snow bank, a huge cloud of snow comes back over the truck. For a while you can see nothing because of this white blanket covering the entire windshield. (Steve later told the family he could hear me sucking in my breath, as I pushed myself back into my seat the first time that happened.)

In addition to keeping the truck on the road and not running over any signs or mailboxes in these conditions, there are two controls between the seats that he needs to operate at the same time that drops sand on the slippery spots after he has crossed over them. As day fades into dusk and then darkness, this "white blanket over the windshield effect" seems to happen more and more frequently. I suppose that it is because the drifting snow is getting deeper on the roads. Sometimes I get the feeling that Steve is driving more by instinct than by sight.

There are several lights on the front and back of the truck flashing steadily. This becomes more noticeable as it starts to grow dark. It gives you the eerie sensation of being inside some science fiction contraption, at least for first time riders it does.

Then there is his cell phone. It seems to ring a lot for someone that I would think really needs to stay focused on what he is doing.

After a while I figured out that he has a special ring for the other driver plowing snow on the other side of the township. Mostly he ignores calls if they are not from the other snow plow. Except one time he answered a call from a friend after the 2nd or 3rd time he had tried to call Steve, "I can't talk right now Dan, I'm driving the snow plow and am in the middle of a big drift. Goodbye." And another one from home about 6:00 pm. Supper was ready and our other grandson and his family were there. "You guys go ahead and eat, save something for us, it is going to be awhile before we are done." (Their unwritten creed seems to be, 'We don't quit until the roads are open.')

Both trucks start on the far sides of the township and work their way toward the middle, making it easier for them to help each other finish up. As they draw closer together, Steve's phone rings more frequently with calls from Merle, the other driver and the conversations go something like this:

"Where ya at?" "I just came off Hog Road and am headed over to Skunk Hollow." "What are the roads like?" Not too bad. Slippery by Sam's barn near County 21, almost drifted in by Snake Creek. What's it like on your side?" "The north-south roads are holding up, but the east-west roads are taking a beating."

We continue on. Indeed, the east-west roads *are* filling up. The wind is relentless. On one road, called Soldiers Lane, Steve isn't satisfied the first time through, so he turns around and takes another run, using the force of the plow, which is stronger than the wing, to push the snow back further, on the wrong side of the road. No choice if he wanted to get the road open.

More calls from Merle. "When you get done where you are, can you come down Lexington Road and clean out the south end?" We do, and when we come back the other direction, somebody's Christmas tree by the side of the road goes flying over a snow bank and into a field as the wing on the truck hits it. When we get to an intersection, Steve turns around to take make another pass to clear the road of snow he couldn't push back far enough the first time. He backs up and makes a third run on part of the road before he is satisfied.

The phone rings again. "When you get done with Lexington, come in behind me on Hickory Highway and clean up what I couldn't get, will you?" Steve's truck is the larger one, so Merle had gotten into some snow his truck couldn't handle.

When this was finished, we headed for the township garage, our work done for today. Merle had arrived shortly before. The two drivers chatted briefly about road conditions, worst spots, a plan for tomorrow, and we headed for home about 7:00 pm for a late supper. Steve had started plowing about 7:00 am I asked him if it didn't take a while to settle his nerves down after that long a day, constantly on alert. He said that sometimes it takes a long time.

Steve called me while I was writing this. He is back in the plow again. He told me about an ice storm they had a few days ago. About midafternoon, he got the call from Merle. "Roads are icing up, we gotta go out and do some sanding." At 11:00 pm they called it a day…or night. By that time it was getting so foggy, it was hard to see. Steve said at one point, he was coming down a hill when the truck got away from him on the ice. I asked him what he did. "Nothing you can do but hang on and ride it to the bottom," he said. Yeah, that must be a hoot, riding a 44,000 pound monster that you can't stop, down an icy hill on a dark and foggy night.

Just another day in the life of Snow Plow Man in the hill country of Wisconsin.

Later…text message from Steve on February 3, 2014:

Goin 2 install hot plate & cot in snow plow. Think Spring.

AN EPIC ADVENTURE

August 2017

The "epic adventure" began when they met at the airport in Fairbanks, Alaska on August 28, 3,200 miles north of Brownsdale. Jason, who had been exploring Alaska for most of the summer, picked up his brother Kevin from the inbound flight at 11:45 pm. Kevin and Jason both grew up here in Brownsdale and graduated from Hayfield High School.

The original plan was to check into a motel and head north early in the morning. Kevin and Jason both agreed that they were too excited to sleep, so after a stop at Walmart for needed supplies, their journey into the unknown began.

Their route took them over parts of the (mostly gravel) Dalton Highway that runs northwest of Fairbanks from a town called Livingood (pop 16) 414 miles to Prudhoe Bay on the Bering Sea, where the Trans-Alaska Pipeline begins. In between is a place called Yukon River Junction, a traveler's stop where the road crosses the legendary Yukon River. There you can purchase fuel, food and a place to rest. Gas is $5.50 a gallon and other services are priced accordingly. Then there is a place called Coldfoot (pop. 10), about halfway to Prudhoe Bay. Jason had filled his tank in Fairbanks and he had a range of 400 miles, which would be *almost* enough to get them to where they were to meet a plane and back to Fairbanks. Gritting his teeth, he topped off his tank at $5.50 a gallon, then they had breakfast and continued on their journey.

If you have seen the TV show called "Ice Road Truckers", then you have seen parts of this road. From Livingood to Prudhoe Bay is a lightly-traveled gravel road. Their destination on this road was a place called Pump Station No. 5, which is just what it says it is, a pumping station on the oil pipeline, with a landing strip on the other side of the road called Prospect Airport, 210 miles north of Fairbanks.

They unloaded their gear for the hunt and waited for a small single engine plane to pick them up and fly them about 65 miles further northwest to a place called Bettles (pop 13). Bettles is where the outfitter they had made arrangements with would fly them out to their hunting camp on a float plane. At Bettles, Kevin, Jason and their gear were taken to a small, old, cozy little cabin for the night. They decided not to have the $35 salmon dinner at the lodge, opting to prepare food for themselves from their supplies.

Wednesday morning they awoke to what was going to be a day of rain-snow mix with 30 mph winds, unfit for flying where they were going.

Thursday morning came with a light drizzle and poor visibility. They still had about 120 miles further to go, some through mountainous areas, to get to their hunting spot in The Brooks Range, north of the Arctic Circle and well north of the tree line. No trees meant no camp fires to warm up or dry out. Food was basically coffee and oatmeal for breakfast, snack bars, peanuts, raisins and jerky for the day and an evening meal of dehydrated food which you add water to and heat up.

Finally, about 11 am a break in the weather allowed them to load up the float plane and head out even though the ceiling was very low. Kevin was in awe when he looked out a side window on their 120 mile flight through mountains to see a wall of granite very near the plane.

Kevin and Jason were surprised to find two hunters at their base camp waiting to be flown out when the plane landed on the lake. They had expected to be located at a place no one else had been, somewhere along the route of the caribou migration south. With a light snow on the ground August 30, camp was quickly set up. The small two-man sleeping tent was set up next to the lake, about 100 yards from the storage tent and cooking area.

A herd of about 100 caribou was spotted on the other side of the lake from the camp. Excitedly, a quick supper was prepared and they headed out to do some scouting for tomorrow's hunt. At that time of the year, the sun doesn't go down until about 10 pm and full darkness is at around 11 pm.

Friday morning, after a quick breakfast of coffee and oatmeal, they headed out to explore the other side of the lake where caribou had been spotted the night before. After spotting about 25 caribou, Kevin and Jason attempted to get within shooting distance, but the caribou eventually spooked and ran off. It is hard walking because the ground is covered with something called "tussocks", which are very similar to what we call "bogs". Either you have to plot a course through them or try to step on top of them, which sometimes works and sometimes doesn't as they grow in wet ground and dry ground and you don't know which you're about to step on.

After more scouting to figure out the best place for an

ambush, they called it quits early and returned to camp. Jason got his fishing rod out and went fishing. He caught a nice grayling on a small Mepps lure, which became supper. As the evenings are quite long, they went back out for an evening hunt. A small bull was spotted, but they passed on that and returned to camp.

On Saturday, they spotted a white wolf in the distance as they hunted and explored. With no cover to hide behind, small gullies around ridges in what can best be described as rolling county were the best bet. From a high ridge, Kevin spotted seven bulls, so they split up, hoping to get in front of them in the draws going around either side of the ridge. One of them passed Jason at a distance of about 275 yards, but he didn't have a chance for a good shot, so let it go.

With a temperature of 22 degrees early Sunday morning, the water bottles in the tent were frozen. Jason said he knocked the ice of his socks and pulled on his wet rubber boots. It is not practical to wear the usual hunting boots because of the amount of standing water in the tussocks they have to walk through. Due to the amount of walking involved in this type of hunting, body moisture is formed in the heavy rubber boots with no way to dry them out. The bottom of his pants were also wet, so he loosened the ice on them before dressing. Sometimes he tried wearing his hip boots, but they were very cumbersome.

After the usual breakfast of oatmeal and coffee, they hiked up to the ridge they had discovered the day before. On the way up, they spotted a caribou that walked by about 50 yards from the spot where they were headed. And it was a whole lot closer to camp than the one Jason eventually shot. This greatly encouraged them to feel that they were dialing in on caribou hunting in this area.

At this spot they watched wolves moving around at a distance and spotted their first grizzly, moving off into another valley. Jason said it was probably the nicest day with the temp getting up to about 50 degrees. By 6 pm they decided to pack it in and head back to camp for supper, when they saw a herd of about 25 bulls, called a "bachelor band," coming down a ridge toward them. They were waiting for an opportunity, but got "winded" and the herd ran off. A migrating herd of caribou can move at 7 mph when grazing and even faster when not grazing.

At 4:30 am Monday, it was coffee and oatmeal in the dark before heading back to the same location as yesterday, with high hopes and great expectations. About all they saw was a grizzly and her cub moving away from them. By 6 pm they were ready to head back to camp. Kevin wanted to try his luck at fishing, and Jason took his .22 rifle to look for some ptarmigan they had spotted earlier, hoping to add some fresh meat to their diet.

As Jason was walking away from camp, he heard Kevin yell, "Jason! Bear!" The urgency in his voice made Jason feel that he needed to go to the supply tent and pick up Kevin's rifle before continuing on to the lakeshore. As he rounded the corner of the supply tent, Jason spotted the grizzly bear on the shore, looking at Kevin, who was standing in the lake not more than 10 or 15 yards from the bear. At about 25 yards from the bear, Jason, with a can of bear spray in his left hand, a .45 revolver in his right hand, and Kevin's rifle strapped to his back, hollered at the bear. The bear turned around and took a couple of steps toward Jason. Jason yelled more and waved his arms, which seemed to spook the bear, causing it to turn and run off a short distance and up a small hill where he stood up on his hind legs and looked back at them, before ambling off.

Jason went up the hill to see where the bear had gone. He had to holler at the bear five or six more times before it finally left the area. Some might wonder why not shoot the critter rather than take the risk of it coming back. Alaska does not look kindly on people who shoot their grizzly bears. You would need to fill out a 10-page report with questions on both sides, then the Alaska Highway Patrol would fly out to the scene and investigate.

Jason returned to the lakeshore and could see the bear walking along on the other side where he had intended to go hunting ptarmigan. He decided to forget that idea, and Kevin felt like he had enough fishing for that day.

Supper was finished by about 9 pm when they spotted a band of caribou moving around a ways off and decided to try for them. Unfortunately, before they got close enough for a shot, they ran off—most likely spooked by the bear, which Jason and Kevin found near their sleeping tent when they returned. More hollering and arm waving finally convinced the bear to leave. It was decided to set up a trip wire alarm around the tent before turning in about 11 pm.

On Tuesday, September 4, they slept in a little bit, due to the late night. After coffee and oatmeal, they grabbed some snacks for the day and headed for a new area near a river where they had spotted a caribou crossing.

Glassing the area after arriving at the river, Kevin spotted a caribou on the other side of the river. Kevin suggested a spot where he thought Jason could set up an ambush and Kevin stayed in place.

After several attempts, Jason finally found a place he could cross the river with only a little water over the top of his rubber boots. Jason then walked up a hill to locate the caribou. He spotted it, but it was now further away.

Deciding on a new place to intercept the bull, Jason started walking toward it. Eventually, he spotted the bull looking straight at him, so he dropped to the ground, covered his head and waited.

Most likely curious, the bull started walking toward Jason. It found some good graze, stopped to eat, and turned sideways to Jason at 180 yards. BANG! 11 am. Now Jason had to figure out how to find Kevin to let him know he had a fine caribou on the ground. He walked up another ridge and finally spotted Kevin looking at him through his binoculars, about a half mile away. Jason held his rifle up in the air and did a happy dance, hoping Kevin would understand. He did, and started walking toward Jason.

Kevin stayed with the caribou while Jason walked back to

camp to get the butchering equipment and packs to carry out the meat. To do this he had to cross the river again, find his pack that he had left where Kevin had been, and then hike through the tussocks, arriving at camp about 2 pm, three hours after he had shot his caribou. Hungry and exhausted, having had nothing to eat since the early morning oatmeal, he knew he had to eat, rehydrate and have a short rest before starting the return trip.

His feet were becoming critical after being wet for three days, so he switched into dry socks, put on his hiking boots, hung his hip boots around his neck, loaded gear and headed back to Kevin. He needed to switch hip boots for waders three times before arriving at Kevin's location about 5:30 pm, pooped. After reenergizing with jerky, peanuts and raisins, came the job of carving and cutting up the caribou for 2½ hours.

At 8 pm they loaded meat and gear onto the two pack frames, each of them weighing about 65-70 pounds when loaded with the caribou meat, and hiked back to camp almost non-stop. They were racing the sun through difficult terrain with no flashlight. Arriving at camp about 10 pm, they still had to switch the meat into special game bags and try to build a small platform out of willow twigs growing along the lakeshore.

They finished about 11 pm, and after a short rest, Jason got up to get food for supper out of what is called a bear locker. He noticed something by their sleeping tent and asked Kevin what he thought it was. "A bear!" he replied. This one was bigger and darker in color than the one Kevin had encountered on the shore when he was fishing. Both of them walked toward the bear, shouting and waving their arms. The bear walked closer to the tent, but eventually turned and walked away. They followed the bear past the tent to keep an eye on him until he faded into the growing darkness.

Setting up the trip wire around the tent, they went back to the cooking area for a very late supper and crawled into bed about midnight.

Kevin was up about 7 am and, stepping out of the tent, spotted a grizzly bear on the meat. He yelled at Jason who got up and joined him in yelling and waving arms at this grizzly as it dragged off most of the caribou.

At this point, Jason said he wanted to make a suggestion to Kevin. "You want to call for the plane to pick us up today instead of tomorrow?" Kevin asked. Jason nodded. Kevin agreed it was a good idea as they were both too tired to hunt another day, and if they did shoot another caribou they would probably have to fight with another grizzly that night.

Making contact with their outfitter was a rather complicated operation. Cell phones don't work in that area. Jason had a satellite phone called an InReach which permitted him to send a text message to his sister Colette who was in Wisconsin at the time. Colette tried calling the outfitter on a land line and got a busy signal for 45 minutes. She finally got through with the message, and the outfitter agreed to send a plane for them. Colette texted this info to Jason.

Knowing that a plane was coming and it was about an hour flight, they took down tents and packed up their gear. As they were doing this the weather deteriorated. The wind picked up, it started to rain and visibility was dropping. They got another text from Colette saying the plane had turned back due to poor visibility.

They sheltered themselves as best they could, sitting together on the ground, using a plastic tarp for a windbreak and pulling it up over their heads.

They wondered, "Now what?" What if no one could get to them before dark and they had to spend the night? What if? What if?

Separately, at one point in Colette's dialogue with the outfitter during the day, he told her he was almost ready to press the red button, meaning he would call the State of Alaska emergency services for help as he had two hunters at risk.

Finally, another text came from Colette that said the outfitter was going to try again and another plane was on the way! In due time they heard the drone of a distant aircraft growing steadily louder. They soon saw the plane appear, land on the lake and taxi toward them.

After their gear was loaded up and they were airborne the pilot of this plane told them that he had to make a stop and pick up another guy. Both Kevin and Jason were puzzled by this, wondering who on earth would be camping out there by himself. They got their answer when the plane landed on another lake and they saw a man standing next to another plane. Kevin and Jason soon figured out the "other guy" was the pilot of the plane that supposedly had turned back, but had developed engine trouble.

Talking to the outfitter about their experience after they had landed safely about mid-afternoon, the outfitter commented that he wouldn't sleep in a tent in that country.

When they returned the bear locker to the Park Service, they were told that theirs was the fourth group of hunters that had reported a bear problem this year.

Jason said that the outfitter offers grizzly bear hunts after the caribou season for $10,000.

Mom and Dad were kept in the loop as this story unfolded. When they learned that the boys were safe, they agreed to forbid "those kids" from doing this again, as it is way too much stress on us old folks.

Somehow, I don't think any of us need to worry about it as I think this was a Once In a Lifetime experience here.

Those who turn back know only the ordeal, but they who persevere remember the adventure. ~Milo Arnold

COMMON SENSE - OUT OF STYLE?

April 2013

Do we still need "common sense"? Should we even try to use common sense anymore? Or have we finally passed enough laws, regulations and rules to guide us and do we have enough enforcers to make sure we follow all these laws, regulations and rules? Maybe it is not practical, or even wise to try to use "common sense" as a tool to make decisions.

Common sense is defined in the Merriam-Webster dictionary as "sound and prudent judgement based on a simple perception of the situation or facts". Thus, "common sense" (in this view) equates to the knowledge and experience which most people already have. Josh Billings, an American humorist quite popular during the civil war period, defines common sense as "The knack of seeing things as they are, and doings things as they ought to be done."

I got to thinking about common sense as I pondered the strange story that is unfolding here in a small town in Minnesota about a little baby boy. I sat in on parts of a two day hearing recently to determine who is best suited to care for this child - the parents and maternal grandparents or the county. I listened as the attorneys were reminded that they could not use the name of the child, only refer to him by his initials, because he is a minor, I suppose. Then the morning after, I read a story about this hearing on the front page of the *Minneapolis Tribune* that used his name, Rico. And I wondered, do we have different rules for different people, or just too many rules?

I am sure that by now you have most likely heard a great deal about that story, as state and local news media have pretty well covered the sad story of a little baby being taken out of his mother's arms by a well-intentioned Human Services person and a deputy sheriff just doing his job, with helpless grandparents looking on.

As a man, I cannot even begin to imagine the emotions being felt by this young mother, barely a woman herself, as two men approach her and take her baby out of her arms, not knowing if she will ever see him again. They ignore her admonition that he has trouble eating from a bottle.

As a parent and grandparent listening to endless testimony by well-meaning people I try to understand the frustration and anger that the grandparents, also well-meaning people with more at stake than anyone else, must have been feeling at that time. And with more personal experience with a certain drug than anyone else in the room. On a video presented at the hearing, I listened to their daughter crying as two men who she thought were supposed to help and protect them take baby Rico out the door.

Some of the laws in use in this little drama came about because we have too many irresponsible people giving birth to babies that are not interested in mothering a baby, the most precious gift from God. I am sure that we have all heard the term, "dumpster babies"…people on drugs throwing their babies into a dumpster shortly after giving birth. Most if not all states have laws in place now, that allow a mother to drop off a baby at a hospital or some other facilities, with no questions asked.

The above scenario is not what we are dealing with here. I hardly know the mom and dad of baby Rico, but I do know the grandparents. They are hardworking, responsible members of this community who own a very successful business here in Brownsdale. It is successful because they made it that way. What little common sense I have tells me that people like this are not going to do something to harm their own daughter or grandson.

I visited with them the other day in their home, in an effort to understand how this happened. Their daughter, who lives with them, is waiting to hear if she will gain full custody or continue to have supervised custody of her son.

He is about four months old now. He is fed by a tube fastened into his stomach somehow. The tube leads to a small box with an electric pump. Any time they move him they need to carry the pump also, being careful not to get the feeding tube or electric cord tangled or caught on something. Rico's grandfather said Rico might have to be fed this way for a year because he had trouble drinking from a bottle. His daughter was breast feeding the baby for two weeks when Rico was taken from her. He was unable to drink from a bottle and she explained that to the Human Services person who assured her "they had it taken care of" or words to that effect.

The people who were supposed to care for baby Rico delivered him to the hospital within a few hours of receiving him because they couldn't feed him with a bottle. The doctors fixed that by inserting the feeding tube. Rico was going to be given the same medicine his daughter had received 22 years ago, a drug called AZT. The grandfather said they were not given the opportunity to explain why they were afraid of the medicine the doctors said they had to give Rico, before the order was signed to remove the baby from his mother's care.

AZT was the same medicine they started to give their daughter 20 years ago, when the second test for HIV was positive, (she was an adopted baby from Romania) and when she grew sicker and sicker they stopped the medicine and she got well. Nine other children under the age of six died from this potent medicine at that time. The grandparents said they told Rico's doctor that if you give that medicine to this baby you will kill him. They gave him the medicine anyway and after having to give baby Rico four blood transfusions due to side effects, they stopped. He is still receiving three different meds. I was told by the grandparents that a baby inherits anti-bodies from the mother and whatever has protected his daughter Lindsey for the last 20 years, would pass on to the baby. Baby Rico was in the hospital for 51 days after being taken from his mother. For the first five days the parents didn't know where there baby was, because nobody would tell them.

The grandparents have had substantial personal financial expense as a result of trying to protect their grandson. They are awed by the moral support they have received from the community. They have received many cards expressing support from members of the community.

The grandfather said, "There is no place else like a small town. The support we have received from the people of the community is just overwhelming. This is a great place to live."

After I left their home, I couldn't help thinking, "How different could this have all been, if someone in a position of authority in this sequence of events had been permitted to use some common sense?" After all, this isn't Germany in the early 1940's with Hitler and his Gestapo, or Russia in the 1950's, with Stalin and his KGB. No, this is America, "land of the brave and home of the free", isn't it?

The end of this sad story: Rico's mother became severely depressed, and the virus that had been lurking in her body for 22 years reared its head and finally killer her. Rico lived until he was about six years old, progressing to the point where he could sit in a high chair if he was tied in and eat some food with his fingers. Then he died.

You should never wear your best trousers when you go out to fight for freedom and truth. ~Henrik Ibsen

AN INCIDENT IN SARGEANT

January 1992

On a cold and blustery day in January 1992, I was in the office of our bank branch in Sargeant (population 78). As I talked on the phone, I could see an individual approach the outer door with what appeared to be a .45 automatic pistol in his hand. He was wearing an army fatigue jacket and a blue stocking cap was pulled over his ears, he had a stocky build. It was hard to determine his age. He stopped and crouched down at the side of the door - as if waiting for someone.

My first thought was, "This can't be happening. What do we do?" I couldn't just wait to see what he was going to do. So I got up, walked around behind the counter and along the wall to the door. There is an entry way in the front of the bank, so I flipped the lock on the inner door, so it would close and lock if I let go of it. From this close, I could see he was a young person maybe between 13-14 years old, about 5'10" with a stocky build. I was still unsure of the gun. I spoke to him in a loud, stern voice and asked what he was doing. He looked up -- surprised – and said he was playing army or something. I asked him what kind of gun he had. "BB gun," he said. "Let me see it," I said in a very authoritative voice. This may sound like a foolish thing to have done. But after 26 years in banking and having been involved in several collateral collections, I have learned that average people in high stress situations don't react like you might expect.

I figured if it was a real gun, I had a 50-50 chance of him doing what I said, because things weren't going according to plan. I kept my eye on the gun as he responded. I planned that if the muzzle comes up, I was letting go of the door, (which would automatically lock) and running for the phone.

However, he opened the outer door and passed the gun in—muzzle down. I looked at it, determined it was a BB gun, and handed it back to him. I suggested he go play somewhere else and returned to my desk and a waiting phone call.

But the story doesn't end there. I was unaware that one of our customers drove up as this boy appeared to be entering the bank with a gun. She also saw something I hadn't seen. Two more boys crouched down behind a car -- with guns.

Now, had this been the typical person used to living in a small town, she might well have stopped at the gas station and asked what was going on over at the bank. She wasn't and she didn't. She was the widow of a St. Paul police officer living on an acreage outside of town -- and she didn't mess around. She went directly to the home of a friend living around the corner, ran in, dialed 911 and reported a bank robbery in progress.

Meanwhile, the man I was talking with on the phone said he was going to send me a fax. Being a small bank, and in the early days of fax machines, we didn't have a separate phone line for the fax machine. So I hung up the phone, switched on the fax machine and told the two tellers not to answer the phone as I was waiting for a fax.

Now, when the Sheriff's department received this call from our customer about a bank robbery, the first thing they naturally tried to do was call the bank. At the bank we stood around listening to the phone ring and wondering why the heck the fax wasn't coming through! When the Sheriff didn't get any answer to his call to the bank, he decided that our customer must be right, and acted accordingly.

About this same time, there was a funeral in Brownsdale, another small town nearby with a population of about 700. Because it was for a man whose son was in the Minnesota Highway Patrol, five cars of officers attended the funeral. You have to understand, we have never had five patrol cars in Brownsdale at one time!

When the funeral was over and they were just leaving town, a call came on their radios that that there was an armed robbery in progress at Sargeant. Since they had about a 10 mile head start on the Sheriff's Department, we had a town full of patrol cars in Sargeant in no time.

One of the patrol cars pulled up across the street from the bank. "Don," one of the tellers called out to me. "There is a police car across the street and I think the officer is pointing a gun at the bank." I looked out the window. She was right. There was a highway patrolman behind his car with his shotgun across the roof of his car, and it was pointed at the bank.

So I stepped outside and called out to him to tell him everything was alright. He said, "Who are you?" I thought, "Oh shucks", (or something like that). I identified myself. And he said, "Come over here". I did -- slowly – my hands well away from my body. I never realized before how ugly a shotgun looks from the business end, when someone is pointing it at you!

He asked for ID, and as I showed him my driver's license I explained to him that it was just kids playing around. Satisfied, he immediately got on his radio, repeating over and over, "They're just kids!"

But by this time, two other patrol cars had stopped in the middle of the road, about a block away. Four officers were already out of their cars running up a side street, with their shotguns at their shoulders! I felt so helpless -- I knew I couldn't run fast enough to stop whatever was going to happen to those kids.

Fortunately, the officers involved had a high degree of professionalism. The kids got so scared they dropped their guns. They were handcuffed, put in patrol cars, and taken to the Sheriff's office where they were questioned and eventually released to their parents.

Later, one of the mother's complained to me. She was upset because the boys got roughed up a bit as they were forced to lay face down in the snow while they were searched and cuffed. I tried to explain to her that those bruises will heal but... if even one of those boys had started to raise his gun to show the officers it was only a toy, he would never have gotten the words out of his mouth.

It was such an unusual chain of events that were laid end to end that day. If there hadn't been a teacher's workshop that day, the kids wouldn't have been out of school...

If we hadn't been expecting a fax at the exact time the Sheriff's Department tried to call us...

If the customer who spotted the boys hadn't been the widow of a big city police officer...

If there hadn't been a funeral that day which brought in cars full of out-of-town police officers...

If...

The absence of any one of these events would have broken the chain. Later, the Mower County Sheriff said he had never seen a set of circumstances that had such a potential for tragedy....

It is a miracle that no one was hurt.

MARBLES

April 2014

I got to thinking about marbles the other day.

When we were kids, we used to play marbles. We had regular marbles, shooters, steelies, jumbo marbles.

I wonder if kids today still play marbles? Probably not. We drew a circle in the dust of a dirt road. That is what most streets in the small towns of mid-America were when I was a kid. It would be hard to play on blacktop or pavement like we have today.

Each of the players put a marble inside the circle and the players would take turns trying to knock each other's marbles out of the circle with a shooter. You got to keep the marble if you succeeded.

Some marbles had a brighter color or fancier design than others, and were more desired.

Sometimes kids with fancier marbles were reluctant to play with kids with ordinary, scruffy looking marbles, like mine, I suppose...

Most kids kept their marbles in a mason jar. A kid with a large jar of marbles had respect. You felt good if you had a lot of marbles in your jar. You felt really bad if you lost all your marbles.

As I was thinking about the game of marbles and the importance of a large jar of marbles, I realized how unimportant and insignificant that is now. But it was really important when I was eight years old.

And then, another thought occurred to me. I think I can see some similarities between little kids and big kids (some would call them adults).

I think you know where I am going with this, don't you?

No, it is not about marbles anymore. When you become an

adult, other things are more important.

Where did you go to college?

What kind of car do you drive?

What part of town do you live in?

What do you do for a living?

Who are your friends? Your spouse?

No, little kids and big kids really aren't so different. They just use different names for their games.

But we still feel bad if we lose all our marbles, don't we?

THE RULE OF UNINTENDED CONSEQUENCES

February 2017

Unintended consequences are outcomes that are not the ones foreseen and intended by a purposeful action. The term was popularized in the twentieth century by American sociologist Robert K. Merton.

One example of this. In the 1960's the Women's Lib movement was started. The term "bra burning" was well known as some women burned their bras in protest (in California I believe, where else?). There were many demonstrations for Women's Rights. They were demanding equal pay as men were receiving for the same work, the opportunity to serve in higher management positions, and to be treated as equals with men in all circumstances.

I actually think the birthplace of this movement goes back to the 40's during WWII. Most of the able-bodied men in the country were in uniform, fighting the war in Europe, the Pacific and various other parts of the world. Women left their homes by the thousands and went to work in the factories, replacing the men who were called to war. They built tanks and planes, bombs and bullets, and whatever else needed to be built. When the war was over, the men who survived came back home and went back to work in the factories.

Many of the women were happy to leave the factories, get married, establish a home, etc.. But not all women felt that way. The fight for equal rights for women has continued to the present time. We now have women fighter pilots, heads of giant corporations and many politicians who are of the female gender including one of the recent presidential candidates. Women have made great strides in their quest for equality.

But has it gone too far? Have we lost our identity between the sexes? For example…

In the military there has been increasing pressure by women to open all combat roles to women and in December 2015 this happened. There are no restrictions to what positions women can apply for.

In June of 2016, the Senate passed a bill requiring all young women to register for the draft (Oh, did you miss that news? Rest easy, it didn't pass in the House of Representatives…yet.) For those of you who don't know, the "draft" is the compulsory enrollment of men into national military service. This ended during the Vietnam War in 1973.

However, all young men between the ages of 18 and 25 are required to register for Selective Service. This registration is the process the government uses to create a list of men that can be quickly drafted into military service in case of a national emergency. Not registering is a felony, punishable by a $250,000 fine and imprisonment for up to five years. Pick up a brochure at your local post office and read all about it.

Sometime after this bill was passed, I saw a news clip on a local TV station. A young woman reporter asked a female army veteran with 17 years of voluntary service if she thought young women should be required to register with Selective Service. "Absolutely," she replied, "if that is what it takes for women to gain equal rights."

I could not help but think that maybe the reporter should have gathered a group of young women ages 17-18, and their mothers, to watch a few movies and then ask them that question. Movies like *The Longest Day*, or *Saving Private Ryan*, movies about the Allied Landings in 1944 on the beaches of Normandy where 160,000 men arrived on the shore in landing craft that day; 10,000 of them were killed, wounded or went missing in action -- on that first day. (I knew a man from Brownsdale, Curt Haukom, who was a bombardier on a B-17 stationed in England at that time. He said that 1,000 4-engine B-17 bombers flew down that beach dropping bombs before the landing, to try to soften up the German army defending the shore.)

Or maybe an interesting movie called *Pork Chop Hill* from the Korean War where Americans suffered 36,000 dead and 8,000 still missing, in a place where it gets just as cold in the winter as Minnesota. Anybody want to sleep outside tonight after reading this?

Or a movie about that miserable place called Vietnam where we suffered 58,000 casualties. Another Brownsdale resident, Dick Spinler, has talked to me about the monsoons, when it rains steady for three months, the hordes of mosquitoes, the flies, and the huge rats that would sneak into your bunker at night and eat the calluses off the bottom of your feet without you being aware of it. And needing to wear your flak jacket every day in the heat and humidity due to the constant shelling. And of men dying because their jeep hit a land mine and blew up. The force of the explosion threw two men out of the jeep. They landed face down in a rice paddy where they drowned because their arms and legs were broken so they were unable to push themselves over to breath.

After watching a few interesting movies about these difficult periods in our nation's history, I wonder if young girls and their mothers would have given that reporter the same answer as the one she got from the woman army veteran who wanted to be in the army? Or maybe we should ask some fathers if it is necessary to expose their daughters to these kind of risks? Isn't it enough that our sons may be called upon to die in a God-forsaken place such as this because our leaders decide it is necessary for "The National Good"?

Who would have thought the drive for Women's Rights would have brought us to this point?

Another example of Unintended Consequences, I think, is the "gender confusion" situation.

There was a TV sitcom in the 1970's called *All In The Family*. The main character was a man named Archie Bunker. Remember him? He was a white working class bigot, very critical of all non-white ethnic groups, of the customs of young people of the day, and of people who were "gender confused" shall we say. It was extremely popular and ran for several years. We all laughed at poor Archie, not with him, because of his extreme prejudice.

Since that time, gradually, and then more often, I could not help but notice that we have reached a point where it is difficult if not impossible now to find a TV program or movie that does not have some part of it portray a gender confused person in a positive way. If you watch for it, you will become aware of it. Sometimes it doesn't seem to even have anything to do with the main story. Just a short scene, almost like a person stopping by to say hi, and then leaving again.

Then we had states, including Minnesota, that made it legal for people of the same gender to actually get "married". Look up marriage in a dictionary. Until recently at least, it was defined as a union between a man and a woman.

As an illustration of how much and how quickly things have changed, think about this. In August of 2008, Barack Obama as a candidate for the presidency stated, "I believe marriage is the union between a man and a woman. Now, for me as a Christian, it's also a sacred union. God's in the mix." And then on February 23, 2011 U.S. Attorney Eric Holder announced... the president has concluded that the Defense of Marriage Act is...unconstitutional...The president has instructed the Justice Department not to defend the statute...(*Citizen Magazine* May 2011)

Early in 2016, the President of the United States issued an Executive Order requiring all public schools to make all bathrooms gender neutral. In other words if a boy thinks he is a girl, he can use the girl's bathroom and locker room and showers. Failure to comply could cost a school federal funding. Fortunately a group in Texas brought a suit against the federal government and a Texas judge has issued a restraining order against implementing this Executive Order until the suit can be heard.

I have read that only 1 or 2% of the population are in this category however over time the LGBT (stands for – Lesbian, Gay, Bisexual and Transgender) folks seem to have gradually taken control of the entertainment industry, the news media and many of the politicians at all levels (this writer's opinion).

When will it be that churches trying to preach the Word of God will have to be careful of what they say or they will be accused of committing a Hate Crime? Don't think so? Check out what is happening in Canada now.

Who could have imagined that Archie Bunker would have brought us this far?

THEN, we have the saddest story of all, about some folks who passed through our lives all too quickly I think. Some of you may remember a story I wrote about four years ago regarding common sense. It starts many years ago, when a young couple who could not have children decided to adopt a baby girl from a far off land. As were the rules of the day back then, the baby girl had to be tested for the HIV virus before coming to America. The test was reported as negative and a young couple in Minnesota happily welcomed their new baby daughter. Later, she was tested again in Minnesota and the test was positive. A new drug was being used to treat young children with this problem. Unfortunately the side effects were deadly for some of the children. The young girl in this story got sick and then sicker. After seeking advice from several doctors the parents found a doctor out west familiar with this drug. He informed them that the medicine was killing their daughter. They stopped giving it to her and she got well. Nine other children under the age of six in the Minneapolis area died from this medicine, according to her parents.

Fast forward about 20 years. A new baby is born. It is a boy. Parents and grandparents are so happy. His mother came from a far off land as an adopted child and even though she seems to be healthy and well she has the HIV virus in her body. Doctors tell her that her baby boy must be treated with drugs including the one she was given as a child. It is the rules. The parents refuse. Doctors report this violation to the Human Services Department, according to the rules they have to follow. The Human Services Department goes to court, and gets an order to remove the child from the parents' custody, for the good of the child, according to the law.

One evening a Deputy Sheriff and a person from the Human Services department, both of them just following orders, come to the home of the grandparents and remove the baby from his mother's arms. She tells them tearfully that he cannot drink from a bottle and must be breast fed. She is told that arrangements have been made to care for the child. They got it covered.

Less than 12 hours later this baby boy is delivered to the hospital by the foster parents, because they can't get him to eat. Doctors solve this problem by installing a feeding tube surgically into his stomach. The tube is attached to a box with a pump and timer that pumped food and medicine into his body at regular intervals. All goes well for a couple days. Then, infection sets in at the incision. Now he needs antibiotics in addition to his other required medicines.

I suppose there is a limit to the amount of medications that a body, any body, can handle but maybe especially a very young, tiny body? The last time I saw him, he appeared to be almost comatose. Eyes wide open, arms outstretched, not moving or responding. I think he was about a year old. The grandparents spent tens of thousands of dollars filing motion after motion with the court, for the mother to get custody of her baby. Their case was always heard before the same judge who had originally signed the order removing him from his mother's care. They finally were allowed supervised custody, meaning someone from Human Services was a frequent visitor in their home, always present when the mother administered the drugs he was required to take.

Finally, the grandparents were exhausted and worn out, their daughter was becoming more and more depressed. They closed a very prosperous business and moved away from a town where they had been so happy, hoping a change would help rejuvenate their daughter. It didn't. She grew more and more depressed, sometimes not leaving her bedroom all day. Her immune system weakened and the HIV virus that had been lying dormant in her body all those years blossomed, took control of her body and she eventually died in her early twenties, shattering several lives.

The father took custody of the baby and as far as I know, he is still not able to function on his own. I think he is about 4 years old now. The maternal grandparents who fought so hard for this little boy and their daughter have not seen him for at least 2 years and do not know what his situation is. How terribly sad.

If somebody along this chain of events would have been allowed to use a little Common Sense, how different this story could have been. Common sense - is defined by

Merriam-Webster as, "sound and prudent judgement based on a simple perception of the situation or facts." Thus, "common sense" (in this view) equates to the knowledge and experience which most people already have. Josh Billings, an American humorist quite popular during the civil war period, defines common sense as – "The knack of seeing things as they are, and doings things as they ought to be done."

The three examples I have presented here, of what I believe are the "unintended consequences" of various courses of action made me think of something else. I have heard people say they believe we are becoming a "Nanny State". What is a Nanny State? Well, the Cato Institute defines it this way: One of the more disturbing trends in government expansion over the last 30 years has been the collection of laws, regulations, and binding court decisions that make up the "nanny state".

Those laws and regulations represent government at its most arrogant. Their message is clear: politicians and bureaucrats know more about how to live your life, manage your health, and raise your kids than you do. Former president Ronald Reagan once said: "Government exists to protect us from each other. Where government has gone beyond its limits is in deciding to protect us from ourselves." Today's policymakers would do well to heed Reagan's words.

Do we have too many laws that control our lives? What say you, dear reader?

THE CHILDREN'S SERMON

September 1997

It was the custom of our pastor to begin each Sunday morning service by gathering the young children around him at the foot of the altar. He would sit down on the step with them and tell them a bible story, asking questions as he went along, to involve them in the story. When you ask questions of children, some of whom are pre-school age, you do not always get the expected answer. Some of these answers would give the congregation a good chuckle and did not seem to bother our good pastor one bit.

On Sunday morning as one of these little dramas was unfolding, something caught my eye across the church, and as I turned my head, I noticed a most amazing thing! All attention was focused on the pastor and his group of children, and everyone had a little smile on their face.

But I saw something more. As I looked across this sea of faces, I saw a teenager with his parents. Earlier, his attitude indicated he was not there of his own free will. I saw an elderly gentleman that had recently lost his wife. There was a young couple that I knew were having financial problems. And there was a woman who suffered greatly with the pain of arthritis. And I *knew* that for one moment, one instant in time for these people, and perhaps many others like them, there was no pain, no hurt, no fear, and no anger as their hearts and minds concentrated on the story our pastor was telling the little children about Jesus.

I have often thought that if I had any artistic ability at all, I would paint a picture of this beautiful scene, and I would name it *The Children's Sermon.*

THE TEA CUP
By Leone

June 2011

My husband and I were married while he was in the Army, more than 50 years ago.

Shortly afterward, he was transferred overseas and ended up in Berlin, Germany, and I returned to my family's farm near Blooming Prairie.

In about six months he had saved enough money to buy an airline ticket for me to join him.

He did not have enough rank to qualify for military housing, so we lived in a very small apartment on the third floor of a German home. We shared the bathroom on the second floor with another military couple.

While we were in Germany we took a trip by plane, train and bus to see some of the sights of Europe.

Our last stop before heading back to Berlin was in a small town in Bavaria named Garmisch. It is located in the foothills of the Alps. We rode a cog train to the top of Zugspitze, the highest mountain in Germany.

On the way back down we got off the train about halfway and walked the rest of the way through some woods, along a road. We had cold chicken and an apple for lunch.

Garmisch was an incredibly beautiful place. Many of the buildings had scenes painted on their sides. We stayed at a military R&R (Rest and Recreation) hotel. It was February, cool and snowy. We walked the streets taking in the sights.

We went into shops looking at many pretty things. In one of those shops I spotted this cup and saucer, which I bought for a souvenir at my husband's insistence. ☺

Somehow, that cup and saucer has survived all the years, and all the moves. Now, when I look at it, I am reminded of two very young, very happy, very naïve, people, so much in love.

And somehow, we have survived all those years as well.

THE CLOCK

January 2002

My friend George has spent the last forty years in a wheel chair.

After retiring from two different businesses that he started, he decided he needed something to do to occupy his time. He taught himself how to fix clocks. George is very handy with tools. You could even call him a skilled craftsman. One day, a friend gave him some nice walnut wood, so George decided to make some clocks.

When I saw what he had made, I knew I had to have one. My clock kind of looks like the front of a little old country church. It even has a bell tower with a little bell in it. For good measure, it has a slim spire on each corner, extending through the roof almost as high as the bell tower. The whole thing stands about twelve inches high. The clock is battery powered, but it has a very audible ticking sound, and strikes melodiously on the hour and half-hour.

For several years it sat on the mantle in our family room. When I retired, Leone and I bought a travel trailer and pickup truck so we could do some traveling around the country. We took the clock along in our trailer, so that we could have a little bit of home with us, wherever our travels took us.

Our first night out on our first trip after retirement found us in a mostly empty RV park somewhere in Kansas. The sound of the clock made us feel at home that cold January night.

During a short stay in Texas, a strong wind came up during the night. Our trailer was shaking and our awning was fighting to be free. Reluctantly, Leone and I crawled out of our warm bed to put up the awning. It was a hard job and we were almost numb with cold when we came back in. The clock cheerily announced it was 3 am.

Our clock kept us company in Florida, where we hid out from the Minnesota winter for a month.

On another journey to northwestern North Dakota, the clock was with us again. This time our objective was to find the land my grandparents had homesteaded in the early 1900s. When I was a child, my grandmother used to tell me stories about their experiences in this harsh, isolated land. This had aroused my curiosity and I have wanted to visit the area for many years. With the help of an old plat map of the township and a picture my cousin had given me, we found the place.

Awesome is the only word I could think of to describe the feeling of knowing I was standing on the land I had heard so many stories about. The buildings were long gone. Nothing but miles and miles of wheat. Almost as desolate and empty now as it was a hundred years ago.

That evening the steady ticking of the clock made it easy somehow, to slip back in time to my childhood. To remember the stories my grandma had told me about this place…

In the winter, a trip seven miles to town for supplies took two days for grandpa to get there and back. Grandma stayed behind to care for the livestock and the two young children they eventually had while living out there. (I don't even want to think about childbirth in this territory back then.) Wolves howling close by the house. She would open the door and fire her little pistol at them to scare them off.

In the summer, prairie fires would occasionally sweep across the land. All the homesteaders would try to stop it by plowing a fire break with their horses and walking plows. Sometimes it worked, sometimes it didn't.

Summer also brought the grasshopper plagues in a dry year. So many they would darken the sky. Eat everything in their path. Nothing stopped them.

Eleven years of this was enough. They sold their homestead and moved to northern Minnesota, shipping their livestock by train. Grandpa rode in the cattle car with his animals, in December.

Memories.

Moving on, our clock marked the time for us, stuck in a snowbank for three days. An early autumn snowstorm dumped 12 inches on Red Lodge, Montana, and closed Bear Tooth Pass. The KOA had planned on closing for the season, but weary travelers kept coming in, seeking refuge. I learned to convert garbage bags into snow boots and Leone did a lot more baking and cooking than she usually does when we are on the road.

The clock suffered its first injury when a rough spot in some forgotten highway brought it tumbling to the floor. Surprisingly, the only damage was to the bell tower. I carefully glued all the parts back together and it looks "almost" straight.

For a variety of reasons, we sold our trailer and pickup. And the clock went back on the mantle.

Last winter we rented a trailer in an RV park in Florida. We missed the clock.

Leone had to make a quick trip back to Minnesota when her mom ended up in the hospital. When she returned to Florida, she had a grin on her face as she carefully unwrapped something she had in her carry-on bag. It was the clock! That night the rented trailer felt more like our place with our clock chiming away.

We decided we weren't ready to give up our wandering ways and camping out in strange places. We have another trailer and truck now.

The clock is securely installed in our new trailer, so that we can be certain it will suffer no more accidents. And it will not get left behind again.

In fact, the clock was with us on our latest outing in our trailer. I like to think of it as our "Early Spring Cold Weather Experimental Expedition to the Leech Lake Area of Northern Minnesota." Temperatures dropped to 16 degrees and …..

But that is another story.

THE BLUE JIG

The 2003 Minnesota fishing season opener - Leech Lake Minnesota

My fishing partner on this opener was my granddaughter Stephanie.

The day started out cool, cloudy and a little windy. I decided I was going to start fishing with a Lindy rig and maybe put on a jig for Stephie. While trying to decide what color to start her out with I remembered Kevin's story about the governor.

The governor fished the opener on Rainy Lake last year. Kevin knew the fellow who was going to be the governor's guide. They had fished together and the fellow was impressed with the amount of fish Kevin caught on a blue jig. It is Kevin's favorite, and if he is jig fishing he always starts out with blue. When the governor and his guide came back in from fishing, Kevin was at the boat landing. The governor had had pretty good luck fishing. The guide came up to Kevin and just said, "Blue Jig".

I decided that if it was good enough for the governor, it was good enough for Stephie, so blue it was.

By the time we got the boat launched at Sugar Point, I could see the wind was coming up, the waves were growing, lots of white caps now. I had wanted to go out to Submarine Island, but forgot about that as soon as we cleared the shelter of the harbor.

We headed north of the harbor entrance to set up a drift along the shore. A lot of other boats out today! We had not been drifting too long when Stephie informed me she had a fish. I looked at her pole, which was bent over. By the time I got the motor into reverse to work backwards, her pole straightened out. She reeled in and her minnow was gone.

Still not sure if she had a fish on or snagged the bottom, I thought we might as well go back and drift through that area again. We had not been drifting too long when Stephie exclaimed, "Grandpa, I've got a fish!" I looked at her pole which was really bent over, and said, "Stephie, are you sure or are you caught on the bottom?" She assured me that it was a fish, so I started working back against the waves.

It wasn't long before I could tell it was indeed a fish. A very nice fish! I got the net ready. I tried to explain to her about not horsing the fish in. I don't think she heard me. She was very intent on getting that fish in. I asked her to bring it toward the back of the boat so I could reach it with my net when the fish got closer to the top. She did this so quickly that the fish actually came to the top and surfed across the waves to me. (That one was really hooked good!) I did manage to net the fish as it was flying by, and got him in the boat. It was a 22-inch walleye! I estimate it weighed between 3-4 pounds.

During all this commotion we had shipped a little water and Stephie expressed concern over the amount of water in the bottom of the boat. I assured her that as long as there was more water outside the boat than there was inside the boat, we were OK.

We continued to drift fish along the shore. Stephie had several more strikes and almost caught a couple more fish, with the Blue Jig. I wasn't getting any action on my Lindy rig.

By noon, we were both getting cold and hungry, so we took a break, loaded up our boat and headed for home.

Talking with several fisherman, and the man at the boat landing at Sugar Point, I believe Stephie did better than 90% of the fishermen on Leech Lake on opening day. By catching that one large walleye. On "The Blue Jig".

I know what color jig I am going to start with the next time I go walleye fishing.

By Don Peterson (also answers to various other names from time to time including but not limited to the following: honey, dear, dad, Grandpa.)

I LIKE TROUT FISHING
(written especially for Andy)
(11th revision)

June 2003

My sister (the one in Texas) asked what was so special about trout fishing.

I had to think about that for a while, before I could give her an answer.

The place where I do this trout fishin' is a lovely tree shaded stream, which meanders through a wooded valley, with tall hills and bluffs on both sides.

These hills are home to deer, turkeys, coyotes and heaven only knows what else. The water is always extremely cold regardless of how hot it is, and it is always noticeably cooler near the river.

A long time ago there was a town nestled at the bottom of this little valley. It was home to about 600 people. It had, among other businesses, a general store, livery stable, hotel, gristmill. Unfortunately when the railroad came through this part of Minnesota and didn't come through this little valley, the town eventually died. Everything is gone now, except for the store and livery stable.

They say that a group of volunteers gathered and trained on a field across the river from the store, before they went off to fight in the Civil War.

Sometimes, very early in the morning, I am the only one on the river. The mist is rising off the water and little fingers of fog curl around the green hillsides. I swear I can smell the smoke from their cooking fires, and hear the sounds of a group of soldiers waking up, starting another day...

It is incredibly beautiful down on the river, with the sun coming up and shining down through the leaves of the trees, reflecting off the water. And so quiet when you are very early and all alone on the river. Except in the spring, when the birds serenade you with their many beautiful songs.

I guess I have been fishing this river for so long, I know where all the trout live, or should live. I think they move just often enough to keep me humble.

And I always know what they are feeding on....yesterday.

Trout fishing as I see it is made up of two parts. Hunting and catching. And, if you approach this most enjoyable pastime with the right frame of mind, you can enjoy the former while having no luck at the latter. After all, you know, just wait until next time.

Trout fishing is pretty much a solitary sport. Maybe that is one of the things that attracts me to it. You can go trout fishing with someone else, but that means that you are on the same river, within a quarter or half mile of each other. You make a few casts, then move on to the next spot. An opportunity to spend some time with yourself. And reflect. Or just enjoy the beauty of nature.

I thank the Good Lord for each opportunity that I have to enjoy trout fishin', as I know the day is coming when I will no longer be able to. Already, I suspect that they are making the eyes in the hooks much smaller than they used to. And the fishing line seems to be a lot thinner. I think they are making it out of some kind of new material that almost disappears once it leaves the end of your rod. And the banks along the edge of the stream seem to be much steeper than they used to be.

Aaah yes, trout fishin'…..

I wonder if they have trout streams in heaven? I sure hope so…..

THE TROUT LURE

October 2007

This spring the Good Lord was kind enough to let me celebrate 70 years of life.

My sister (the one from Texas) wanted to give me something to celebrate this momentous occasion, as I was the first one in our family to reach this age. The fact that I was the oldest child probably had something to do with it.

She said her husband was in Cabela's there in Texas, so she asked a clerk what kind of lure would be good for catching trout. He picked one out and assured her it was a good trout lure. It was so thoughtful of her to want to do that.

When I finally got a chance to go fishing this spring, I took her lure along. I was excited and anxious, when I got to the stream, as I usually am. I have fished this area for so many years, it always comes as a surprise to me to find myself so filled with anticipation as I approach the stream.

The sun had not been up too long. It sparkled and danced across the riffles of the stream surface, in some of the open areas. There were pools of dark shadow under the canopy of the trees. The strong scent of spring blossoming flowers and shrubs was especially pleasant this still morning. The birds were all busy doing their spring thing. Several different species were all greeting the new day with their own song, at the same time. And no one else is here! I feel sorry for anyone who isn't me this morning!

I really didn't want to start the season using a new and strange lure for the first time. I decided I would start with a plain old, usually reliable night crawler. I know many people scorn the use of live bait to fish for such a noble species as trout. To those people, I say, try it sometime, let me know how it works out for you; then we will talk about it some more.

Anyway, this morning it seemed that the trout were scorning my nice night crawlers that I was offering them. And they didn't much care for some tasty looking wax worms either.

I switched to my trusty tube jigs. They always catch trout. I started with the yellow and white one. My son Kevin sounds skeptical when I tell him I have good luck using tube jigs to catch trout. I don't care, they work for me a lot of the time.

Hmm. Not interested in yellow today. I tried the next most popular color. Red. Not a nibble. Green. Not today.

Well, gee. The trout are being picky today, aren't they? I looked through the tackle I had brought along to see what else I could try. I had a tried and true Mepps that had caught a lot of trout, but hadn't been used for a long time. I tied it on and moved to a new spot. Not even a little hit.

I was starting to feel a little frustrated. I decided to try the trout lure my sister had given me to mark my 70th birthday. I kind of hated to use it. It had been sitting in its box on my desk, since I received it. I could look at and think how thoughtful she was.

I moved to another spot. A wide spot in the stream, that had a deep hole.

I took out the trout lure, the one my sister had bought from some sales person in Texas. What do they know about trout down there, I wondered. I thought they mostly had catfish and rattlesnakes down there.

I carefully tied it on my line and gave it a cast. Well, it casts pretty good, a good feel on the retrieve. I moved slightly and cast to another spot. Nothing. I moved just a little and cast to another fishy looking spot. I was getting a little more comfortable with the feel of it. Still nothing.

I moved down carefully, almost to the bottom of the wide spot in the stream. I cast across and back upstream as far as I could and reeled in rapidly. The lure stopped. Nuts, I thought. I am snagged. But wait a minute, the snag is starting to move! And line is peeling off my reel.

I started moving upstream, trying to follow along the streams edge. This was a really good fish and I had to be careful not to let him break my line. I tried to slow him down with my thumb on the edge of the reel. He turned and went across the pond to the other side. As I increased the pressure on the reel, he jumped out of the water, shaking his head, trying to throw the lure. What a beautiful fish! As he sank back in the water the line felt slack. Did I lose him? What is happening? No, he is coming back down stream. Frantically, I turned the handle of the reel as fast as I could, to take up the slack. He went past me like a bullet, going farther downstream this time.

As the line tightened up, he leaped out of the water again, his tail splashing on the surface of the stream. He shook his head, spit out the hook, and he was gone.

Gone???

Gone!!!!!

My memory banks were not able to process the information as rapidly as my optical sensors were transmitting it.

I felt shaky. I sat down on a nearby stump, to give my pulse rate time to return to somewhere near normal. I needed time to think, to realize what had just happened.

After a while, I got out my pocket knife, cut off the lure and slowly returned it to my creel. This was not a lure to use on an everyday basis. This is a lure to be held in reserve and used only on special occasions.

What a memorable day on a lovely trout stream.

Thanks to my sister.

Some men fish all their lives without realizing that it isn't fish they are after. ~Henry David Thoreau

THE TROUT STREAM

July 2015

I went trout fishing yesterday. I went back into an area I usually only fish in the spring because weeds and young willows grow up so bad, so I usually quit fishing that area about mid-June. Yesterday, I thought I should just try it to see.

There is a large hole, probably the largest one on this stretch of the stream, before it connects with the Root River about a mile further down. And then there are two smaller holes beyond the first one that I really like to fish.

Well, by the time I got to the first hole, I knew I didn't have it in me to go any further. The weeds and young willows were growing as high as my head and much higher in many places. And so thick, one could barely tell where the trail is. The temp was about 80 and no breeze at all. And this hole is in the sun, no shade at all. I was beginning to question my sanity in choosing this place to fish today.

Fortunately the sun was at my back so I thought I might as well give it a try as long as I am here.

The water was crystal clear and I could see a lot of fish lying on the bottom. Of course they all spooked when I approached the edge. I knew if I was patient and stood very still they would drift back in, and they did. I made a few casts to various places, and then as I lifted my rod ever so gently to move the worm, a trout just hit it! A good fish I had on and I was careful not to try to bring him in too fast as I work with a very light line, colored on my end so my old eyes can see it, and clear on the fish end so…

It looked like I was going to be able to bring him in. The stream bank is not the best here. It sits about a foot above the water, so it is hard to reach down to net a fish. There are some underwater, almost flat rocks a little under the water, so I decided to try to step down on one of them to be in a better position to net the trout. As I tried to feel for the rock with my foot, and keep an eye on my line, suddenly I found myself going head over heels into the stream, and going down into the deeper hole beyond the rocks. My hip boots filled quickly with water. Thankfully I was able to somehow scramble back up on the shore, thinking I'll bet my good fish is gone now.

Surprisingly, he was still on the line. I landed him, then I laid on my back as best as I could and lifted my feet in the air to drain some of the water out of my hip boots. I could not take them off or I would have never got them back on, wet inside and all.

I decided I might as well stay there and fish, maybe I would dry out some. So I sat on the small piece of shore where I had flattened some of the weeds with all my thrashing around. My feet were in the water, on the rock I had been trying to reach, and I was able to fish that way, carefully. As I did so, I noticed another fishing line right at the water's edge. THAT is what had put me in the water. I didn't slip, I tripped on that blasted line. It was a very heavy line and tight at both ends. I can't imagine anyone fishing for stream trout with that heavy a line. I tried to pull it loose to see what was on the end, but I couldn't break it with my hands. I took my knife out and cut it. If I hadn't sat down I would have never noticed it and could very likely have taken another tumble.

Fishing was good. By the time I decided I had better try to get up, I had caught six or seven trout and did an "early release" on a few more. I kept five, and two of them were the largest trout I have caught this year. My best day of the season, so worth the effort!

When I finally stood up, I could tell I was stiffening up, but it had been a good day. And now it was warmer than when I had come in here. On my way back out, I met up with a hole in the trail that I have met up with before. So many times in fact that that hole and I are on a first name basis. The first name of that hole is "*darn*" (or something like that). It seems like it is always covered with a little grass and I never see it. Usually I stumble a bit and keep going, but guess I was getting tired and this time it got me and I went down. When I tried to get up, one foot caught on some weeds and I went down again. I decided maybe I should just stop here and rest a bit, which I did. Thankfully I made it back to camp without further incident.

Fortunately I had dry pants, underwear and socks at the trailer. Quite a day. A good day.

Today, I am nursing a sore knee so am just going to take it easy.

THE BLIZZARD BUCK
(as told to me by Kevin)

Deer camp November 1998 - An isolated area of far northern Minnesota

Dad and my brother Jason had just left for home after a weekend of hunting together. They took with them a nice eight point buck Jason had shot the day before.

I fixed myself a quick lunch and put another log in the stove before I left. Our deer camp is a large outfitters tent with a small wood stove for heat and room enough for our three cots. A table made from an old wood palette to hold our camp stove and a gas lantern hung from the ceiling pretty much completes the camp.

It is set up in a small stand of balsam, a short distance off an old fire trail, in very large woods. There are a lot of bogs and wet ground in this area.

I tied a portable stand onto the back of my pack, grabbed my rifle and headed out. I wanted to check out an area I had noticed during a pre-hunt scouting trip. And it gets dark early up here. Especially when it's heavily overcast, like this afternoon. Must be some weather moving in.

The area I wanted to check out was about a 45 minute hike from our camp. Through a short piece of woods, across a thick stand of young poplar, wade the standing water almost to the top of my boots, along what must have been an old logging trail, at one time. Past the long abandoned cutter's shack, finally higher ground, only to drop down to the edge of the cedar bog. From here I started leaving pieces of blaze orange trail tape on branches to mark my way. Very small pieces not easily seen unless you are looking for them.

The cedar bog is a fantastically beautiful, eerie place, on the brightest of days. And this is not one of those bright days. Early afternoon now, and already gloomy in here. Cedar trees growing right up out of the water. Some with twisted, gnarled trunks, look like they have been there forever. The roots bulge up out of the water like the swollen knuckles of arthritic hands. Bits of dried cedar branches, other stuff, float on top of the water. Very silent in here, other than the sound I make as I move as quietly as possible through the water, sometimes almost boot high again. Not much sunlight gets in here on the best of days. Hard to move in a straight line, sometimes necessary to bend over slightly, to get under the branches. This is a really good place to use your compass.

I finally reach the high ground I wanted to check out and start looking for signs. I am not disappointed. Lots of deer traffic back here. Many tracks, some rubs, a couple scrapes, in a heavily wooded area. I can't help wondering how long it has been since another human has passed through here?

I finally find a spot that looks good. A corner where two deer trails come together. Off the trail a bit is a good sized spruce. I work my way up it about 15 feet, cutting as few branches as necessary, and installing steps where needed. I found a near perfect spot to attach my portable stand, cutting a few spruce branches so I can look down both trails without being seen.

After quickly cleaning up the area of sticks and leaves so I can slip into my stand quietly the next morning, I head back to camp. It is now past five and what little daylight we had is gone, but I am satisfied with the location and stand I put up. I believe it has some great potential. As I approach the cedar bog I realize I must have taken a wrong turn somewhere and will have no hope of finding the trail markers that I had put up on my way in. Time to get out the old compass. I am not lost. I am just not sure of where I am. Logic tells me that if I stay on a northerly heading, I should eventually come out on the abandoned winter

167

logging road east of our camp. This works and I must admit that it looks pretty good when I get back to familiar territory. A turn to the west and a short while later I see the welcome site of our camp nestled in between the spruce. No welcome glow of light from the tent or pleasant smell of wood smoke from our stove as I approach tonight.

I started a fire to warm the place up and prepared a quick supper of leftover stew and biscuits as the tent warmed up. I heated some water for a cup of tea, which I drank sitting next to a crackling fire in our small stove. Morning comes early in our deer camp, and I am getting that delightful warm, drowsy feeling that only comes from some serious physical exertion, so by 8:30 pm I roll into my sleeping bag, knowing I will soon be asleep.

The alarm wakes me at 4 am. Rain is pattering softly on the roof of our tent. The temperature had been hanging in the 20's, but it must have warmed up a bit. It was very tempting to roll over and go back to sleep. Reluctantly, I overcame the temptation and climbed out of my sleeping bag. A few small pieces of kindling on the dying embers in the stove quickly brought it back to life. It warmed up nicely as I cooked coffee and heated water for our standard deer camp breakfast. Instant oatmeal and bread. Quick to fix and it sticks with you. Sandwiches made and put into my pack along with some cookies, raisins, candy bars, an apple, to sustain me while I am gone. My small thermos of coffee and a water bottle complete my packing.

I head out of camp at 5 am Pitch dark. Raining softly but steadily. No wind and the air has that heavy feeling about it. Maybe I should bring a portable radio next year so I can catch a weather report? My eyes grow accustomed to the dark, as I pick my way through woods and swamp, using my small flashlight as little as possible. I can move a little faster because the rain and dampness muffle the sound, but the darkness slows me down.

I like to be in my stand about an hour before daylight, to give everything a chance to settle down, and I arrive at the tree with my stand in it and am quietly settled into it, a little before 6 am.

Now the wait begins. And so does the time to think.

Think about the preparations for the hunt. The excitement that slowly builds as equipment is gathered, checked, loaded. The scouting for just the right place to put up stands. Three days, and nothing so far. Will this be the day? I really like this location. The rain should have muffled any sounds I made coming in and washed away any scent I might have left along the trail. And it will stay dark longer this morning, because of the overcast. Not too cold. Yet.

Think about hunts past. The deer I have shot, and the deer I have missed. Hunting partners. Where we stayed. Weather conditions. Fellowship. Good times all, in spite of heat, subzero conditions, snow, rain.

Think about my life. Job, family, God. Things I am glad I did, and things I wish I would have done differently. Who was it that said "we get too soon old and too late smart"? Oh yeah. Steve Chapman wrote a book, *A Look at Life From a Deer Stand*. Lots of food for thought there.

About dawn, the rain gradually turns to snow. It must be getting colder. Slowly everything turns white. Pretty. And quiet. Boy, is it quiet. No birds chattering. No squirrels scolding me.

Really still.

8 am. No sign of anything yet. Maybe the deer are hunkered down to. I eat a cookie and pour myself a cup of hot coffee. Snow seems to be getting a little heavier. It is starting to build up on the branches of the spruce tree I am in. I should be camouflaged pretty good by now.

9 am. Still nothing. It is definitely snowing heavier now and the wind is picking up. Patience is a virtue, but it is hard to put into practice. I know from experience that deer will move around mid-morning, so I am determined to stick it out for a while.

Shortly after 10 am, I spotted a deer on the trail to my right, that seemed to have just suddenly appeared. (How do they do that?) He was walking slowly up the trail toward me, munching on tender, new growth branches as he came. He stopped, looked up, (what a rack!) turned his head from side to side, and then left the trail. Not fast, as if frightened, but slowly, and continued to graze his way through the woods. If he continued on his path, it would bring him across my front, about 75 yards out. Hopefully, he would pass through an opening in the trees so I could get a clear shot.

I waited patiently. Well, OK, not so patiently. But I waited. It looked like he was going to cross a nice little clearing directly in front of me. Slowly, I raised my rifle. Yes! I centered my scope slightly above and a little behind his left front leg, and fired. Snow that had been building up on the overhanging branches fell, obscuring my vision. When it stopped, I couldn't see the deer. I was positive I had hit him.

Now the real wait began. I looked at my watch. 10:20 am. I made myself sit still for 10 minutes. I stood up. I had been sitting pretty still for over five hours. The cold and dampness were starting to get to me. Slowly, and with some difficulty I started the climb down out of the tree. Dad always said I shouldn't put my stand up so high. Maybe he was right. Everything was wet, I was very chilled. Hard to work my way down through the spruce branches, with my pack and rifle. After what seemed like a very long time, I finally reached the ground.

With my rifle at the ready, I slowly walked toward where the deer should be. Snow seems to have let up a little bit, but the wind is picking up. Maybe the snow is done. I can see some brown through the brush. As I get closer, I can see the rack and start to get excited -- 10 points, very thick tines, a good spread. This is the largest deer I have ever shot, and he is a beauty. Large bodied. A lot of meat.

As I quickly dress the deer, I began to think about how I am going to get the deer and my gear back to camp. It is going to be a very long haul, by myself, over some rough terrain.

I decide to take down my stand, and go back to camp, get into some dry clothes, leave everything at camp, and come back for the deer.

I arrive back at camp about noon, throw a few sticks of cedar in the stove and have a nice, warm fire going in no time. As the tent warmed up, I got out dry clothes and changed, standing close to the stove.

Then I made a nice lunch of bacon, eggs, and some fried potatoes, all washed down with a fresh pot of coffee that I had brewed.

I was just finishing up, when the flap of the tent flew open and my friend Dick stuck his head in. Dick has a hunting shack about a half mile deeper in the woods. "Where's your deer," he asked as a greeting. I told him with a big smile on my face, giving him all the details. "Well, let's go get it," he said. Now there is a true friend. Not everyone would volunteer for the job that lay ahead of us.

It was starting to snow a little heavier again and the wind seemed to be increasing as we left camp. And the temperature was dropping.

By the time we reached the deer, snow was accumulating on the ground, the wind was really starting to moan through the tree tops, and we had some serious snow coming down.

After a short rest to catch our breath, we attached two drag ropes to the deer and began the laborious task of dragging it out of the woods, back to camp. For a short while, the snow helped us, making it easier to drag the deer. Until we reached the cedar swamp.

Now we had a problem. Parts of the roots of the cedars grew above ground. These were covered with water, making the whole mess pretty slippery, and then there were the low hanging branches. We tried to tie up his feet and put him on a pole to carry him out that way. That didn't work because of the low hanging branches. Finally we adopted a procedure of lift, carry, drag, as we stumbled and twisted our way through the trees in the swamp.

We didn't realize how much harder it was snowing until we came out of the swamp. The wind was steadily increasing as well. We made pretty good time dragging the deer along the snow covered trail until we came to the portion of old logging road that was under water. Then we tried to carry the deer using a pole, with mixed results. The water was almost to our boot tops in places, we were growing tired, and it was starting to get dark earlier than usual due to the overcast. The tops of dead trees started to come down with a crash from time to time, from the weight of the heavy wet snow and wind. (widow makers, we call 'em.)

We finally reached the familiar fork in the trail. It was a welcome sight, as we knew there was not far to go now. It was almost 6 pm and full dark when we finally reached camp and got my deer hung up.

The tent was starting to sag from the weight of the snow, as the fire had gone out in the stove and it was cold inside. I quickly lit a fire, and we removed some of the snow from the roof of the tent carefully. We realized now that we were in the middle of a full scale blizzard. More tree tops were coming down, with a sound like a gunshot as they snapped off. Dick wanted me to come with him and spend the night in the shack. At least it had a wood roof. I believed that if I stayed in our tent and kept the fire going, the rising heat would melt the snow as it hit the roof and our tent would be OK. If I left it, the weight of the snow would most likely collapse it by morning.

Reluctantly, Dick left me to tend to his own shack. It was dark, snowing heavily and the wind was blowing like a hurricane, but Dick is an excellent woodsman, and I knew he would make the trip OK. Fortunately, the subzero temperatures sometimes associated with a blizzard had not set in...yet.

After Dick left, I made myself a supper of this, that and the other thing. While I was eating, I heated some water on the wood stove, for some tea to help me make it through what I believed was going to be a very long night.

Supper done, I settled into the chair next to the stove, to drink my tea and listen to the wind raging through the woods outside. Occasionally, the lantern would swing wildly from its hook in the ceiling, and I would hold my breath and hope everything was going to hold up.

I put another log on the fire and reflected on the day. It certainly had been an exciting and event filled one. The biggest buck I had ever shot! A blizzard. How fortunate I was to have a good friend like Dick. Don't know how I would have gotten the deer back without him.

The food I had eaten and all the exercise I had had were starting to have their effect on me, and in spite of myself, I was growing very drowsy. I opened the flap of the tent to check the weather. Still snowing. Still blowing.

I returned to my chair by the stove, and after a while, started to doze off. The sharp report of another tree snapping off nearby brought me wide awake again. Boy, is that wind howling out there. A good thing we set up our tent in the shelter of this small grove of balsam, to help break the wind.

By 10 pm all the exertion and excitement of the day was really starting to catch up with me. I finally gave in and crawled into my sleeping bag, clothes and all, after loading the stove with wood for the night. I slept fitfully for a couple hours, awakened every so often by the sound of another tree going down.

At midnight I crawled out of the sack, and went outside to check the snow. It was still snowing hard, wind blowing and getting colder. The heat from inside the tent was working, keeping the snow from piling up on the roof of our tent. Satisfied, I checked the fire in the stove, added more wood, and returned to my bunk.

I must have dozed off again, and slept really sound this time. The next thing I was aware of was that I was awake, and there was no sound. Total quiet. The wind had stopped. I turned on my flashlight and looked at my watch. 4:30 am. The storm must be done.

I stepped outside for a look. It looked like we had quite a bit of snow. It was drifted up in places, and the trees were hanging heavy with snow. Going to be interesting getting out of here today.

I got a good hot fire going in our stove to dry out the tent as much as I could. While the coffee was cooking I made myself a real good breakfast this morning.

Dick showed up some time after daylight. Between us, we got our gear loaded. Using our chainsaws and shovels, we cleared a path through the downed trees and snow. We eventually made it to the highway and headed for home. And the end of a most interesting hunting trip.

We learned later that the area had received 10 inches of snow, and wind gusts up to 60 mph.

May your trails be crooked, winding, lonesome and dangerous, leading to the most amazing view. ~Edward Abbey

SPIRITS OF OLD MEN

November 2018

In ancient Norse mythology there is a tale that tells of the spirits of old men that dwell in certain trees deep in the forest. I have always been a little skeptical about this (I am not so sure about Bigfoot either), but on a recent hunting trip to far northern Minnesota I think I may have met one of those tree dwellers.

My deer stand is near a large cedar bog, a favorite place for deer to hang out as it is cooler in the summer and warmer in the winter. It was abnormally warm during the hunting season this year, and the deer just were not moving.

It was late morning of the second day. I had heard only two shots this morning. The deer watching was incredibly slow. I sat there staring at a large cedar tree in front of my stand. Slowly I began to realize I could see what looked like the face of an old man in the moss on the side of the cedar. I could clearly see his one eye with a distinctive black pupil, a large knobby nose, a very bushy, grayish looking mustache. His chin was clearly visible as well as some rather scraggly looking long hair partially covering one ear.

I was becoming bored with the deer watching, so I started a conversation with the tree dweller in front of me. It turned out to be a rather long conversation. I noticed that he didn't have much to say, *but he sure was a good listener.*

Artwork by Leone A. Peterson

IS THERE A GOD?

April 2019

Think about it.

The Bible has over 40 authors spanning 1,500 years, all with a consistent message.

Some interesting facts that I gleaned from a book titled *Dinner with A Perfect Stranger*:

Christ's crucifixion is historically documented, not only by early Christians, but also by Non-Christian historians of the time. Throw that out and you have to throw out everything you know about ancient history.

The Dead Sea Scrolls, among other things, prove the reliability of the Hebrew Bible. And you have over 5,000 early manuscripts written by Non-Christian authors, that validate the New Testament. You have what the authors wrote. It's up to you what you do with it, but you have what they wrote.

If God doesn't exist, you have the problem of Design. We live in an orderly world where Spring is followed by Summer which is followed by Fall, followed by Winter, rather than a world of Chaos. How did that happen to happen?

There is a well-known English mathematician named Roger Penrose who helped develop the Black Hole Theory, among other things. He calculated the odds of a cosmic accident producing this orderly universe at "one in a hundred billion, to the one hundred twenty-third power." And that is just the macro universe. He omits the design complexity of biological life. Cosmic Accident. I think he is referring to what used to be referred to as the Big Bang Theory. We don't hear much about that anymore. Some folks believed that all life was created by two meteor type objects accidently running into each other in space and creating life. I tried looking it up on the internet and all I get is references to an old tv show.

I have long thought that if I had another life to live, I would like to become a biologist. I think plants are so interesting. Many years ago, I knew a teacher that worked as a crop hail insurance claims adjuster in the summer months. He knew his plants. Take the corn plant for instance. The growing point doesn't come out of the ground until the fifth leaf stage. If a late frost would kill the leaves when there are only three or four out of the ground the plant would survive. At an early stage in the life of a corn plant, you can cut open the stalk and find a very tiny ear of corn, fully formed. It is my understanding that at that time the plant has already decided on how big that ear is going to be, how many rows of kernels, etc., when that little ear is only 3-4" long. I think something in the corn plant at that stage of growth makes a decision based on the amount of food and moisture available to the plant at that time. How does it do that?

As the corn plant continues to grow eventually there will be a tassel at the top of the plant and tiny silks will emerge from the top of each ear of corn. At the proper time the tassels will open and pollen will drift down over the corn field. Some of the pollen may land on the ears of corn on that plant, but most of it will land on the silks of neighboring plants, moved by the breeze through the field. And the ear clings tightly to the stalk, straight up. As the plant matures the ear will gradually bend over until it is hanging almost straight down, so the kernels of corn are protected against the elements, and so those kernels can produce the next crop.

And then there is the soybean plant. As the plant grows it produces leaves and then pods in which the beans will grow. At a certain point in the life of this plant, the plant will decide, based on the food and moisture available at that time, I suppose, on how many pods it can support, and will actually stop sending nutrients to certain pods. These pods will then dry up and fall off so the rest of the pods can produce seed for the next crop. Oddly enough, this process is called "aborting" these pods.

I believe all the plants have their own story to tell, if we would just look into it.

Louis Pasteur, a renowned French biologist in the 1800's said, "The more I study nature, the more I stand amazed at the work of the Creator."

In the New Testament of the Bible, the Book of Romans 1:19-20 says "Since what may be known about God is made plain to them. For since the creation of the world God's

invisible qualities - his eternal power and divine nature –
have been clearly seen, being understood from what has
been made, so that men are without excuse."

But enough about plants.

Let's talk about the sky, stars and planets, constellations.

For many years I have enjoyed watching the stars at night
and looking for the various constellations. Some I have
been able to identify and some I cannot. One of my
favorites is called Orion, The Hunter. If you are not familiar
with it, it is a constellation with stars aligned so that it
resembles a man, with arms outstretched shooting a bow
with an arrow at a bear. Strangely enough, it is in the fall
that you can see Orion the Hunter in our area. October,
November, if you look up in the southern sky about 6 in
the morning, he will be almost due south. And it is still dark
enough at that time so you can see Orion. (I can see the
man and bow but I have never been able to identify the
bear.) There is another constellation to the right of Orion
called Pleiades that passes through our area ahead of Orion.

Then there is The Big Dipper, with the end of the dipper
pointing to the North Star which has guided travelers across
the barren wastelands and oceans wide since the beginning
of time, long before the compass or this thing called a GPS
was discovered. There are so many constellations, all with
their own purpose - some to guide you in travels and some
to declare the time of the year. Remember, there was even a
time before calendars.

If we go back to the beginning, in the Old Testament
Book of Genesis 1:14, it tells us "And God said, 'Let there
be lights in the expanse of the sky to separate the day from
the night, and let them serve as signs to mark seasons and
days and years.'"

And in the New Testament Book of Mark 8:18 it says, "Do you have eyes but fail to see, and ears but fail to hear?"

In the Old Testament book of Amos 5:8 he makes reference to these two constellations. "He who made the Pleiades and Orion, turns blackness into dawn and darkens the day into night." Think about it. We can see Orion somewhere between 5 - 6 am and after that will come the dawn. And Pleiades will come with the night.

Good and Evil are often referred to as Light and Darkness, aren't they? A coincidence? You decide.

Psalm 19:1-6 declares "The skies proclaim the work of His hands, day after day they pour forth speech, night after night they display knowledge. There is no speech or language where their voice is not heard. Their voice goes out into all the earth, their words to the end of the world." In other words, the entire world can see the skies and understand what it is telling them. More so then, perhaps, than now, because we have all these electronic gadgets.

Is there a God? One God? Our God? What do you say?

Psalm 14:1 tells us that "A fool says in his heart, there is no God." And Psalm 10:4 says it another way, "In his pride the wicked does not seek him, in all his thoughts there is not room for God."

Mark Twain said, "What I don't understand about the Bible doesn't bother me nearly as much as what I do understand."

ABOUT THE AUTHOR

Don Peterson grew up in the small town of Blooming Prairie, MN and with his wife, Leone, raised a family of five kids in the nearby small town of Brownsdale. He discovered at a young age that through reading he could learn and travel to wherever his mind and a good book would take him.

He has a natural curiosity about people, places, travel and history that form the foundation of his writing. His work life has taken him down many paths including army photographer, professional photographer, milk man, banker, real estate broker, insurance agent, landlord, entrepreneur, banking consultant, and journalist.

His personal life is full as he enjoys traveling with his wife and spending as much time as they can with their growing family that at last count also included seven grandchildren and 15 great-grandchildren. Along with fishing and gardening he is active in his church and community, and enjoys chronicling life's events as they pass him by.

When an old man dies, a library burns down.
~An ancient African proverb

AVAILABLE AT:

Gas 'n Go - Brownsdale, MN

Sweet Reads - Austin, MN

Mower County Independent - LeRoy, MN

Blooming Prairie Library, - Blooming Prairie, MN

OR ONLINE: